CALLED TO HIS SUPPER

The Biblical Eucharist

by
Penny Livermore

Michael Glazier, Inc.
Wilmington, Delaware

First published in 1978 by Michael Glazier, Inc.,
1210A King Street, Wilmington, Delaware 19801

Library of Congress Catalog Card Number: 78-50782
International Standard Book Number: 0-89453-089-5

Printed in the United States of America

Contents

II. The New Testament

Explanation...

This infant book has been fathered, mothered, and nourished by the Eucharist. It grew to completion through an awareness of how so many among God's 'little ones' are hungering for the life-giving Bread which Jesus gives, but know it not. For, though at every Mass we exclaim 'Happy are we who are called to His supper!', we do not really know what it is that we say. I have written this book to help others (as I have been helped) to know more fully the meaning of this Supper and why we are to rejoice on being called to it.

It seems to me that there is a widespread need for more familiarity with the Eucharist so that 'going to Communion' may be far more for Christians than a routine obligation or a pious practice. I felt that there has been a lack of emphasis on its biblical background. For it is in the Scriptures, with their manifold allusions to bread and wine, that we can learn to appreciate (and begin to grasp) the Bread and Wine which are Jesus' own Body and Blood.

And so, in these pages, I have ferreted out from the Bible those texts which I feel are rich contributions to an understanding of the Eucharist—whether it be called 'Communion' or 'The Lord's Supper' or 'The Mass' or whatever. Aside from those New Testament passages which are accepted as direct references to this Eucharist, my choice of the selections and my 'eucharistic' interpretation of them is purely subjective. I pretend neither to make 'pronouncements' on the texts nor to accommodate them. I simply wish to share insights from them which have been helpful to me before the Communion Table.

My format is as follows. Each section, which deals with one specific text, unfolds in three differing and complementary ways: the scriptural passage itself, a brief and general exegesis of it which includes personal meditation, and a sonnet (in varied rhyme schemes) inspired by this text. For the sake of logical convenience, the passages are arranged in the order of the books in the Bible. But, although they are interrelated, they are not continuous and may be read in any order.

It is hoped that this small book will help all 'little people' like myself—my 'brothers and sisters in the Lord' who have been called to His Supper—to find that this Communion in the Bread and Wine is truly a *Eucharistia:* 'Thanksgiving!.

P. L.
Feast of St. Thérèse
1977

1. The Old Testament

MELCHIZEDECH
(Genesis 14:18—20)

*And Melchizedech, the King of Salem, brought out bread
and wine. He was priest of God Most High. And he blessed
Abram and said,*

> *'Blessed be Abram by God Most High,*
> *maker of heaven and earth.*
> *And blessed be God Most High,*
> *Who has delivered your enemies into your hand!'*

* * *

Jesus has given us the Bread and the Wine. But ... it was
first, is, and remains ... bread and wine. He has given us
holy Food which is (we believe, though it be mystery) His
body and His blood. But here, at the beginning of our
reflections upon this Food, we are glad to be reminded that
it is, simply, food. He became flesh, He lived as man, He
gave us that flesh to eat. It is good to know that we remain
as men with the need to eat that our flesh may be sustained. Without grasping this human, down-to-earth reality,
earthbound as the clay of which we are made, we cannot
grasp the greater reality of the Eucharist—heaven-sent gift
from the Potter who shapes this clay.[1] Without grasping the
humanness which reaches day-after-day for a wooden or
earthenware vessel filled with wine or milk beside a loaf of
bread, we cannot understand the imperishable treasure of

Bread and Wine held within the earthen-ware vessels into which He has shaped us.[2] This is why we begin with Melchizedech.

Here is a figure who at once is associated with the One to come after him—the Person at the end of all the passages in the Bible foreshadowing the Eucharist. But, this figure remains at the beginning, and a beginning there must be. Melchizedech, 'my King of Justice', king of Salem (Jerusalem of old)—the king who went forth to meet Abraham and blessed him in the name of his own God, God Most High! We are not sure of the original date and interpretation of this singular narrative in Genesis, nor of the identification of this king. We do know that he was taken as a messianic figure who later came to signify the ancient Jerusalem origin of the priesthood, a model for the ideal priest-king of post-exilic days.[3] And, we are most familiar with Melchizedech through the way in which the New Testament author of Hebrews finds him a 'type' of Christ. Like Melchizedech, Jesus is both Priest and King. Just as scripture neither mentions Melchizedech's family nor gives details of his life, so too the Son of God appears as 'without father or mother or genealogy', with 'neither beginning of days nor end of life.'[4] As High Priest, Melchizedech entered into some sort of agreement or covenant both with God and Abraham. But, Jesus is 'the surety of a better covenant'.[5]

However, even though it is not mentioned in Hebrews, it is a further bond which perhaps most closely joins Melchizedech and Jesus. For, Melchizedech brought forth *bread* and *wine,* offered *bread* and *wine* to Abraham. And whether or not this had to do with a 'covenant meal' or a sacrificial rite, we cannot help associating it with the Eucharist. Indeed, even without any 'theological overtones' or ritual significance, we associate Melchizedech's gesture with Jesus because it was, at heart, simply a gesture of friend-

4

ship. For both the king of Salem and our King 'not of this world'[6] have taken what is humble, most ordinary, and earthbound in human life—bread and wine—in order to say, 'I call you my friend!'[7] Spoken by Jesus, these words fill our clay vessels with the Bread and Wine of His Love.

* * *

[1] Isaiah 64:8
[2] 2 Corinthians 4:7
[3] Psalm 110:4
[4] Hebrews 7:3
[5] Hebrews 7:22
[6] John 18:36
[7] John 15:15

5

MELCHIZEDECH

Melchizedech, priest-king: who
this man of Salem (peace) and why should we
recall and hail him? Just apparently
because, a man of God, he had no true
earthly parents or because, a ruler,
he was royalty—hence, in the company
of Jesus? Even more, since offered he
the eucharistic sign—bread and wine?

Yes, Melchizedech means all of these. . . .
But also, something simpler which the eye
of littleness can see: These gifts he rendered
from the ordinary—grapes and wheat
cupped upon a wooden plate. And like
Jesus, he brought Love . . . as a Friend.

MANNA
(Exodus 16:13-15; 31)

In the evening, quails came up and covered the camp. And in the morning, dew lay round about the camp. And when the dew had lifted, there was on the face of the wilderness a fine, flake-like thing, fine as hoarfrost on the ground. When the people of Israel saw it, they said to one another: 'What is it?' For they did not know what it was. And Moses said to them, 'It is the bread which the Lord has given you to eat'. . . .

Now the house of Israel called its name 'manna'. It was like coriander seed, white, and the taste of it was like wafers made with honey. . . .

* * *

They could not believe it; they disbelieved for joy! A multitude famished in the wilderness—famished for bread, for beauty, for breathing and living sign of the Love which had led them already through the Exodus from Egypt. . . . A multitude hungry and parched with no promises of green oasis of relief, but only hungering, more hungering. . . . Then, suddenly, upon the barren brown-grey mountains and rocks and sand, there lay gracefully pulsing, white beauty: bread! Crystal as dew come down within the night, refreshing as rain (rain in desert places), gentle as soft snow mantle (warm snow)—no wonder, no wonder the generations of Hebrews (and Christians) ever afterwards were to

7

call this a 'miracle'. And, it *was* a 'miracle' in the purest sense, because God's miracles are His making use of every-day things to meet the needs of His creation. In this case, it is thought, He marvellously fed His people with a bread-like substance produced by the leaves of a tamarisk plant or an insect that lives upon them. We are familiar with the events of the story. But perhaps we are not quite as familiar with the sheer beauty of the narrative as it is told in Exodus—the wonder of the Israelites at this 'fine, flake-like thing', white as seeds and sweet as honey wafers.

But, even more significant than the event with its por-trayal are the words with which Moses answers the people's amazed questions: 'What *is* it?' . . . . 'It is the bread which the Lord has given you to eat'. *Here* was the 'miracle'! Quite apart from the descriptive beauty of the scene or the tremendous practical import that the starving could eat their fill, there is the fact that they were in *need*. They were in need—and God did provide, He *did* provide. It need not have been bread in a wilderness that was the substance of this 'miracle'. The point is that Yahweh did not abandon His people: He stepped in and delivered them, confirming the deepest credo of Israel.

'As for me, I am poor and needy;
    but the Lord takes thought for me. . . .
Though I walk in the midst of trouble,
    He preserves my life. . . .
And though I take the wings of the morning
    and dwell in the uttermost parts of the sea
    or desert,
even there His hand shall lead me. . . .

For, He provides my food—*anything* I may need.
    He always provides my food. . . .'[1]

8

Here, then, is the 'manna miracle'. And so, we can understand why this 'bread in the wilderness' has been seen as a symbol of the Eucharist. The 'multiplication of the loaves and fishes' (which Jesus performed in a 'lonely place apart') has been compared, even in literary structure, to the Exodus feeding. The comparison is all the more fitting in that, at the time of Jesus, one of the 'wondrous deeds' expected of the awaited Messiah was a repeat of the manna gift.[2] Jesus himself contrasts the manna with the True Bread: the Jews thought that their forefathers, eating manna in the wilderness, were fed on heavenly bread; Jesus points out that they died in that desert, whereas *He* is the true and life-giving bread from heaven.[3] And the mysteries of both Exodus and Eucharist are gathered into the apocalyptic reference to 'hidden manna'.[4] But, perhaps the most beauteous comparison can be made more simply. This 'fine, flake-like thing' upon the ground becomes the sweet, wafer-thin Bread at the Communion table slipped upon our tongue, into our heart.

* * *

[1] cf Psalm 40:17, 138:7, 139:9f, 111:5
[2] cf John 6:30f
[3] John 6:30-34, 48-51
[4] Apocalypse 2:17

9

MANNA

'What, Moses, what is this fine
flake-like thing—like hoarforst on the ground?
It seems a white robe has hushed the sound
of our lamenting, blanketing our whined
cry for bread with a whispered sign:
the wilderness is filled with round
wafers—snow laid on the parched, brown
mountains, water from the rocks' mine.'

'Manna, children, bread—it is the bread
Yahweh has given you to eat. Take
freely . . . but, be mindful why He gives:
amidst your desert places, you are fed—
He provides! His own hands bake
your Bread, nourishment for all that lives.'

THE WORD SO NEAR
(Deuteronomy 30:11-14)

'For this commandment which I command you this day is not too hard for you, neither is it far off. It is not in heaven, that you should say, "Who will go up for us to heaven, and bring it to us that we may hear it and do it?" Neither is it beyond the sea, that you should say, "Who will go over the sea for us, and bring it to us, that we may hear it and do it?" No, instead the Word is very near you. It is in your mouth and in your heart. All you need do is carry it out.'

* * *

The book of Deuteronomy is often considered mainly a compendium of legalistic prescriptions mingled with the command to obey them. Indeed, it has been identified with the 'Book of the Law' found in the Temple during Josiah's reign in 622 A.D.[1] But, at the same time, Deuteronomy is rich in sensitivity to Yahweh's love for His chosen people and to their obligation to thankfully return this love through fidelity to His law. In this passage, Moses, to whom the book's discourses are ascribed, has just indicated the ways in which God will restore and prosper His people. All they must do is keep the commandments as contained in the Law and turn to God with 'all their heart and soul'. And how is it possible for them to do this? Because, Moses assures them, God's commandment or word is *not* something

11

distant or indistinct in heaven or on earth, but is very near at hand. 'It is in your mouth and in your heart, so that you can do it.'

This is one of the Old Testament texts which, in God's eyes, is pregnant with meaning for the New. The original author, speaking in Moses' name, is testifying to the nearness of the *Torah,* the indisputable clarity of its precepts as they had been interpreted and set before the Israelites throughout the centuries. But the christian reader of the text, as even Paul realized,[2] perceives in it an extraordinarily precise and vivid testimony to the Incarnation. The 'Word' of which Moses speaks is Jesus Himself. It is God's word which did not remain too 'hard' and inaccessible in 'heaven', nor too distant 'over the sea', but instead became embodied in His Son to walk this earth. For 'the Word became flesh and pitched His tent in our midst.'[3]

Yes, through the Incarnation, God's word *is* very near; we need not 'cast about' for it. And, it is not 'too hard' for us—whether it be His commandment or His Will—because in Jesus it becomes a sweet yoke and a light burden.[4] He offers us His friendship as Saviour and His own Love-command to enable us to do God's Will. But, it is the concluding words in this text of Deuteronomy which point to how this Word comes closest of all, though the author could not have even conceived that what he wrote was such literal truth. Yes, the Word *does* enter our mouths, rest upon our tongues, and become one with our very flesh and blood. It—He—enters through His own Flesh and Blood in the Bread and the Wine.

* * *

[1] 2 Kings 22:3-13
[2] Romans 10:6-8
[3] John 1:14
[4] Matthew 11:30

THE WORD SO NEAR

'God—Father and Creator—far
away, we murmur fearing. When we pray,
how can He hear or care what we say
hidden where He seems chilled and star-
distant? And we weep beneath this hard
saying: if His Word (unbodied) stays
behind the sky, the sea, is there a way
He comes to us, embodied, where we are?'

'Yes, incarnate! Lo, this Word—no,
one need not bring it to you, heaven-sea
searching far. It is . . . flesh-near,
sweet warm breath just below
your hands—Bread communion kissing Me
into your lips and hearts: I am here!'

ARISE AND EAT, ELIJAH!
(I Kings 19:4-8)

Elijah went a day's journey into the wilderness, and he came and sat down under a broom tree. And he asked that he might die. He said: 'It is enough. Now, O Lord, take away my life, for I am no better than my fathers.' And he lay down and slept under a broom tree.

And behold, an angel touched him and said to him, 'Arise and eat.' And Elijah looked around. And behold, there was at his head a cake baked on hot stones and a jar of water. And he ate and drank, and lay down again. And the angel of the Lord came again a second time, and touched him, and said, 'Arise and eat, or else the journey will be too great for you.'

And Elijah arose, and ate and drank, and went in the strength of that food forty days and forty nights to Horeb the Mount of God.

*   *   *

Life is not easy; life is very real. Our sincerest faith in God and our most loving acceptance of His will do not spare us this hardness. (Indeed, 'those whom I *love* I reprove and chasten',[1] says Jesus Himself.) Our most intimate union with Him does not insure against those desperate moments when we feel we have 'lost' Him: 'You have wrapped Yourself in a cloud so that no prayer can pass through.'[2] But, this little episode in Elijah's life shows how *God* never 'loses' *us*, how *He* it is who holds us fast in His communion and strengthens us to go onwards in our journey. Indeed, it ultimately shows how He strengthens us with the perfect communion: His Bread.

Elijah, the boldly determined prophet, was crushed. His campaign to re-establish the pure worship of Yahweh in the northern Kingdom seemed to have failed. His arch-enemy Jezebel, the Phoenician princess who had seduced Israel into the Baal cult, had warned him to flee for his life, and he escaped to Beer-sheba at the southernmost tip of Judah. It is a poignantly vivid and human picture which the narrative then presents: the fugitive Elijah sinks exhausted beneath a broom tree, convinced that his prophetic mission had failed, and hence beseeching God to end his life. Then, as so often happens at such a moment of despair, sleep came. . . . And lo, upon awaking, he found refreshment near his head—a cake baked on hot stones and a jar of water. The Lord had provided for him, the Lord had not forgotten him even though Elijah had felt ready to give up His service! God was inviting him to eat and drink, so that he might be strengthened for the journey which lay before him! Because, as the next part of the narrative shows, Elijah is making a pilgrimage to Horeb (or Sinai), and there God shall speak to him as once He spoke to Moses. And so, Elijah ate and drank of what was provided for him, and he found that this did indeed give him the strength for his long journey to God's mountain.

How often we too have felt like Elijah, whether it be in his having to flee or his weariness or his disillusionment. We all have our life-journey; in some form or another, it is always a pilgrimage to the mount of God. But, the ordinary food which God provided for Elijah has a deeper significance for *us*. The cake and the water become the Bread and Wine. This food of Himself which Jesus offers to us is the only real strength we have for our journey. And lo! When Elijah reaches Horeb and the conventional 'theophany' or appearance of God is described (as a means of expressing their meeting), it was *not* from the lashing wind or the earthquake or the fire that God communed with Elijah. It was from a 'still small voice.'[3] And this too is our Communion: the most wonderful Word God has ever spoken—His Son— all hushed in the whisper of a still small bread-wafer resting gently within us.

* * *

[1] Apocalypse 3:19
[2] Lamentations 3:44
[3] 1 Kings 19:12

ARISE AND EAT, ELIJAH!

Broom bent shadows, loomed leaves
about Elijah's head, as he clung
mourning with the prophet's cry wrung
from him: 'Lord, it is enough. Seize
my life from me—let me die! My knees
quail beneath the mission once sung
in brave flame, now silenced from
my faint-embered weakness. . . .' Came sleep.

'Awake, Elijah, rise, eat! Take
Life anew, arise, awake! The tree
bent caressing leaves about his heart,
morning fired stones to warm a cake
before him, light a water jar. He ate,
drank . . . and sang! This Bread—his prophecy,
strength for journeying to the Mount of God.

THE BRIMFUL CUP
(Psalm 23)

The Lord is my Shepherd: I shall not want.
He makes me lie down in green pastures.
He leads me beside the waters of repose.
He restores my soul.
He leads me in paths of righteousness, for His name's sake.

Even though I walk through the valley of deep darkness,
I fear no evil.
For You are with me.
Your rod and Your staff, they comfort me.

You prepare a table before me in the presence of my
    enemies.
You anoint my head with oil,
my cup overflows.

Surely goodness and kindness shall be with me
all the days of my life.
And I shall dwell in the house of the Lord
for ever.

* * *

The Shepherd Psalm! How familiar are the words about
the green pastures and the still waters (or 'waters of repose',
as the Hebrew says), the comforting rod and staff . . . and,

yes, the overflowing cup. All the images in the psalm express God's 'goodness and kindness', His loving Shepherd's care for each tiny lamb in His flock. The picture of the 'cup which overflows' (or, is 'brimful') conveys the idea of abundant blessings, of all the 'good things'[1] which Yahweh provides in feeding His hungry flock and gathering the lambs against His breast.[2] It suggests thirst quenched with a living stream pure and refreshing as those still waters.

And yet, tranquil and fulfilled (and close to God) as was the Hebrew psalmist, there was One yet to come who would fill our cups (however humble their size) still more richly and refreshingly with God's Love . . . because He was God Himself. 'If any man thirst, let him come to Me and drink!'[3] Here is the Good Shepherd: Jesus. But, first He himself had to become a Lamb—a small babe-lamb whom other shepherds with their flocks came by night to worship, and a Paschal lamb who drank the cup of His Father's will for Him . . . to be slain.[4] But, through that death the Lamb became the Shepherd who guides us to springs of living water,[5] and that Cup became the Blood-Wine with which our own cups overflow.

* * *

[1] Luke 1:53
[2] Isaiah 40:11
[3] John 7:37
[4] 1 Corinthians 5:7
[5] Apocalypse 7:17

THE BRIMFUL CUP

'My cup overflows: Yahweh—
Shepherding—has led, laid me down
in green pastures, where the silent sound
of waters lullaby my lone day
to rest inside His breast-fold away
from night's cold shadows. And the grass I found
tender shelter for my earthen-brown
cup—humble, thimble-sized, but staying
filled, because Yahweh is kind.' 'Come,
though, drink of yet a richer flow
from your thimble vessel, living sign
of God's goodness. Here, his fleshed Son . . .
who emptied once His cup of death to show
your own is filled with Resurrection: Wine!'

SWEET TASTE
(Psalm 34:1-10)

I will bless the Lord at all times;
   His praise shall continually be in my mouth.
My soul makes its boast in the Lord.
   Let the afflicted hear and be glad.
O magnify the Lord with me,
   and let us exalt His name together!

I sought the Lord, and He answered me.
   He delivered me from all my fears.
Look to Him and be radiant,
   so your faces shall never be ashamed.

This poor man cried, and the Lord heard him.
   He saved him out of all his troubles.
The angel of the Lord encamps around those who
   fear Him.
   He delivers them.

O taste and see that the Lord is good!
   Happy the man who takes refuge in Him!
O fear the Lord, you His saints,
   for those who fear Him have no want.
The young lions suffer want and hunger,
   but those who seek the Lord lack no good thing.

*   *   *

Here is the invitation, the heartfelt plea, of a 'poor man' who has known the meaning of God's deliverance. Here is a psalmist whom God has saved from all his troubles. He has reason to begin his song declaring that praise and thanksgiving will always be on his lips, and he has reason to end with the certainty that Yahweh will never fail those who shelter in Him. For he affirms the sweetest mystery of God's love (and the one which the 'wicked', the self-righteous, most refuse to acknowledge or experience): 'The Lord *is* near to the broken-hearted and saves the crushed in spirit.'[1] And he can make this affirmation because his own heart has been all but broken, his own spirit all but crushed . . . and yet, he has known the tender mercy of One Healer, Uplifter, and Saviour. Wonderful, wonderful are the good tidings which this psalmist has to share: 'Let the afflicted hear and be glad!' The tidings that to seek the Lord in the midst of fears is to be delivered from them, that to look towards *Him* amidst anguish of body or spirit is to receive the radiance of His own countenance upon our faces. And why? Because (in contrast to the 'beasts' who 'want and hunger' because *their* search is for 'bread alone', as it were[2]) to truly seek just *God* is to find Him,[3] and to truly look to *Him* is to 'lack no good thing.'

And so, all but overwhelmed by the goodness of God to him, this 'poor man' (whose affliction—like all suffering—could be described as a lack or hunger for something) could find no more expressive way of proclaiming this merciful Love than through the image of 'tasting sweetness' (and, in the concrete mode of Hebrew thought, this is an invitation to envisage *real* food on a real table with all the human warmth and enjoyment associated with that). It is all the more fitting an image in that, as with food, so with the Lord: an actual mouthful, 'taste', also implies a *little* bit only—and this is all that is needful to find out that He truly *is* sweet.

Yes, he knew, our psalmist, of the Lord's goodness and sweetness. Yet, he did not really know. Yes, he had found a way of saying this through the human language of taste; yet, he knew not what he said. For, he knew not One Word who was to come after him and fulfill his own words. He had spoken in concrete Hebrew imagery, intending that we picture ourselves actually feeding on the Lord. But, he knew not how this *could* be . . . nor how fully it *would* be. . . .

For, through what has come to pass since, man can—and must—'live by *Bread* alone': *the* Bread, Jesus Himself. He, who could never crush even a bruised reed,[4] was to be the perfect Uplifter of the crushed in spirit, the true Healer of the broken-hearted, the final Deliverer of all captives.[5] He was to be . . . *the* Saviour. The food and drink He came to give was real food and drink which would leave man without hunger and thirst.[6] Once a man tastes it, takes it into his lips and mouth and limbs and heart, he knows for sure: the Lord is *very* near, the Lord is sweet![7] How can this be?

We need not ponder. We need but hear the good tidings He himself is. For Jesus asks (and strong His invitation . . .): 'Come to Me! Take and eat—do not be afraid, for it is I!' O, He knows (is He not man?): it may not always seem what *we* would choose, this food—just a pale bread-wafer and a single sip from a wooden cup of wine so faintly red that it would seem the white milk of babes![8] Ah, but strong His invitation . . . to table-fellowship with *Him*.

Let us come, try, taste, and see—how sweet, how good! As if, as if all the loving kindness of the Lord Himself were in this Bread and Wine—yes, as if the goodness that we find so sweet to taste were *He*!

* * *

23

[1] Psalm 34:18
[2] Deuteronomy 8:3
[3] Jeremiah 29:13
[4] Isaiah 42:3; cf Matthew 12:20
[5] Isaiah 61:1ff; Luke 4:18
[6] John 6:35, 55
[7] Deuteronomy 30:11-14
[8] 1 Peter 2:2

SWEET TASTE

'The Lord is sweet, the Lord is sweet—O, hear,
all you afflicted ones, be glad and sing
with me a new psalm! I bring good tidings—
taste of loving kindness: He is near
the broken-hearted. Rising hope He brings
the crushed in spirit—healing in His wings,
Sun—Saviour! Taste—the Lord is here—

good, sweet . . . as bread and wine upon
our tables!' So the old psalmist called,
the true Food awaiting unaware.
For where the sweetest germ of wheat—beyond
human, yet confirmed bread of man? All
God tasted in the small Wafer Prayer!

TABLE IN THE DESERT
(Psalm 78:1-4; 12-20)

Give ear, O my people, to my teaching;
   incline your ears to the words of my mouth.
I will open my mouth in a parable;
   I will utter dark sayings from of old,
things that we have heard and known,
   that our fathers have told us.
We will not hide them from their children,
   but tell to the coming generation
the glorious deeds of the Lord, and His might,
   and the wonders which He has wrought. . . .

In the sight of their fathers He wrought marvels
   in the land of Egypt, in the fields of Zoan.
He divided the sea and let them pass through it,
   and made the waters stand up like a heap.
In the daytime He led them with a cloud,
   and all the night with a fiery light.
He cleft rocks in the wilderness,
   and gave them drink abundantly as from the deep.
He made streams come out of the rock,
   and caused waters to flow down like rivers.

Yet they sinned still more against Him,
   rebelling against the Most High in the desert.
They tested God in their heart
   by demanding the food they craved.
They spoke against God, saying,
   'Can God spread a table in the wilderness?'
He smote the rock so that water gushed out
   and streams overflowed.

Can He also give bread,
or provide meat for His people?'

* * *

Psalm 78 is a long psalm, but it hides within its length and its vast catalogue of events a few treasured words—yes, like laden tables found unexpectedly in the wilderness. This is an important psalm in the scope of biblical theology. It is an 'historical' psalm revealing how the Israelites valued the handing down of tradition from father to son. In this way, children of forthcoming generations might learn of God's goodness to their forbears and hence never forgot to obey His Law in their own times. The psalmist proclaims that he is going to 'utter dark sayings from of old.' He will not keep hidden from his children the 'glorious deeds of the Lord' which were told to him as a child.

And so, throughout the rest of the psalm, he describes the 'wonders' which God has wrought on behalf of Israel—from His delivering her from Egypt to His choosing David 'from the sheepfolds' to be the shepherd-king of His people. However, the psalm recounts not only God's merciful deeds. It tells even more of His people's response to them, a response which was frequently 'stubborn and rebellious', lacking in steadfastness of heart and faithfulness of spirit.[1] Indeed, the speaker dwells on this rebelliousness of his forefathers with a definite intention in mind. He emphasizes the way they grieved and 'provoked the Holy One of Israel' and 'did not keep in mind His power'[2] —in order that the next generation, the 'children not yet born', would *not* make the same mistakes. Now Yahweh's most loving redemptive act on behalf of Israel was the Exodus, a deed forever engraved on her consciousness as the

27

supreme moment of His choosing *this* people. Thus, it follows that Israel's most heartless, ungrateful response to Yahweh was her 'rebellion' in the desert following that Exodus—a deed equally engraved on her conscience.

At that time, Israel's querulous 'murmuring' was a craving for the food of Egypt again. 'O, that we had meat to eat! We remember the fish we ate in Egypt for nothing, the cucumbers, the melons, the leeks, the onions, the garlic. . . .'[3] It was also the people's lack of faith that God could feed them in the desert. This rebellious doubting which is recorded in the historical narratives of the Pentateuch is expressed poetically in our psalm when the people question, 'Can God spread a table in the wilderness?' That is: can God possibly feed such a multitude as we when there is obviously no food here? But, He *does* feed them. Despite their faithlessness, He does feed them. He 'rains down' manna and quail upon them.

And we, too, have our 'deserts', the barren places in our lives when we may 'crave' a meat which is not God's will for us at the moment[4] and doubt that He can nourish us at all. And, given the real 'manna', the true 'bread from heaven' in Jesus,[5] the Wafer seems so frail. It seems so impossible to think that this could be His flesh. We too wonder how this could ever be food for us! But, we taste . . . and soon see: food, real food,[6] upon a table spread before us in the presence of our desert foes.[7] And soon our wilderness blossoms with the white rose of this Manna-Bread.[8]

* * *

[1] Psalm 78:8
[2] Psalm 78:40-42
[3] Numbers 11:4f
[4] John 4:34

[5] John 6:44-51
[6] John 6:55
[7] Psalm 23:5
[8] Isaiah 35:1

TABLE IN THE DESERT

Waste-land—wilderness—but can
God possibly ever spread
a table here, provide water, bread?
Why, rock the only taste! Man
cannot survive this hostile, barren sand
where even shepherds fear to seek dead
lost sheep. . . . So how can God have said
'I shall feed you desert wheat—manna'?

By His voice (come down from heaven)—'it is I!'
Rejoice: the naked wilderness shall bear
a virgin blossom, and a Shepherd take
lost sheep upon His shoulders by
the desert's still waters, to prepare
a Table—and the Living Bread break.

THE BEST OF WHEAT
(Psalm 81:6-10; 16)

'I relieved your shoulder of the burden;
* your hands were freed from the basket.*
In distress you called, and I delivered you;
* I answered you in the secret place of thunder;*
* I tested you at the waters of Meribah.*

Hear, O My people, while I admonish you!
* O Israel, if you would but listen to Me!*
There shall be no strange god among you;
* you shall not bow down to a foreign god.*
I am the Lord your God,
* who brought you up out of the land of Egypt.*
Open your mouth wide, and I will fill it. . . .

I would feed you with the finest of the wheat,
* and with honey from the rock I would satisfy you.'*

*   *   *

'But My people did not listen to My voice. . . !'[1] Our words about the 'finest of the wheat' and 'honey from the rock' (once more familiar through the Benediction liturgy) must be seen in the context of the psalm in which they occur. It is an unusual psalm because Yahweh Himself is speaking. And it is all the more powerful because what He says reveals His infinitely tender—and unrequited—love for His

30

people. In contrast with the third-person narrative of Psalm 78, here it is Yahweh who recounts His 'saving deeds' on behalf of Israel. He speaks through the mouth of a prophet-psalmist who uses poignantly beautiful images.

'I relieved your shoulder of the burden;
 your hands were freed from the basket.
In distress you called, and I delivered you;
 I answered you in the secret place of thunder. . . .'[2]

Yes, in all their distress, God delivered His people and unfailingly sustained them. But, 'My people did not listen to My voice!' It is a cry of anguish wrenched from God Himself, a cry even more sorrowful when joined with His yearning Love: 'O, that My people would listen to Me!'[3] And why, why does He so long for them to turn—to return —to Him? Why, because He is waiting. He is waiting to feed them—to fill their open mouths[4] with the finest of the wheat and with honey from the rock.

But, they refuse. They refuse because they do not really know the nature of this food with which God wants to feed them. They do not know, even though year-after-year they come to the Temple to offer the firstborn of their cattle and baskets filled with first-fruits of the earth—what *they* considered the choicest and 'best of wheat.' They do not really understand, even though the very words they speak at that ceremony derive from the ancient *credo* about their 'wandering Aramean' forefather who eventually became a great nation, which God then released from Egyptian bondage to lead into this land of milk and honey.[5]

But, quite apart from their innate refusal to 'hear' Yahweh, perhaps there is a more understandable and excusable reason for their not knowing about the food He wished to give them. And this was that God Himself had not yet revealed the true nature of this food—the Wheat of His Love. He was waiting. Precisely because He knew that His people could never come to see it on their own or without being able to touch and taste, He was waiting for the moment when that Love was to take on warm flesh—and Bread—in His Son.

And so, we who come afterwards really 'have no excuse' if we fail to respond to God's yearning for us to listen to Him. For, the Food with which He would feed us has spoken personally of who He is: living Bread who sustains us and relieves us of our burdens (by placing *His* sweet yoke upon our shoulders).[6] It is ultimately *He* whom the Father meant by the finest of wheat and honey promised to His people. To refuse His invitation 'Take, eat!' awakens something in Him still more moving than His Father's cry, 'Would that you would listen . . . O, my people, what *have* I done to you? . . .'[7] For, Jesus is man, and He can be heart-broken unto tears. 'O, my people, how often have I yearned to gather you to myself as a mother hen gathers her chicks beneath her wings . . . but, you *would not let* Me!'[8]

* * *

[1] Psalm 81:11
[2] Psalm 81:6f
[3] Psalm 81:13
[4] Psalm 81:10
[5] Deuteronomy 26:1-11
[6] Matthew 11:28-30
[7] Micah 6:3
[8] Luke 13:34

THE BEST OF WHEAT

Harvest-tide—Hallelujah! You
have offered glad Thanksgiving to Yahweh—
good things rained upon your way
lit by His sun passing through
the seed's seasons. You have gathered to
the threshing floor ripe grain, laid
at the Temple door baskets weighed
with grapes . . . and animals . . . your first fruits—

joyed choice! Because this food, your best,
you consecrate to God. Yet . . . come,
take of His own harvest . . . when you meet
the Husbandman of Kingdom Come, the Breast
(where sucked His Son) feeding you with honeyed-
milk mingled with the best of wheat.

THE FOOD I NEED
(Proverbs 30:8)

Feed me with the food that is needful for me!

*   *   *

'Feed me with the food I need'—a small verse, yet saying so much! A simple verse, concerned with man's most elemental need for food. Yet, this simplicity contains all the real 'elementals' of man's life; it voices a cry for the only food that can satisfy his deeper heart. The book of Proverbs is a motley collection of 'sayings of the wise', including disciplinary teachings and exhortations for 'right conduct'. The words of various sages have been linked together. Because all of them use conventional literary forms of the wisdom genre, it is difficult to distinguish the thoughts of one from those of another. But, in this little snippet of a passage, somehow a distinct personality emerges—one who (by contrast with the impression given by many a 'wise man') knows his own dependence upon Yahweh. And so, he prays for 'two things' (numerical lists are a characteristic of Proverbs), and he desires both of them in order that he may never 'offend' his God. He prays that all deceitful falsehood be removed from his lips. And he asks that he be given neither poverty nor riches—neither of the two extremes—but only enough with which to live comfortably. 'Feed me, O Lord, with just how much is needful for me each day—no less, no more!'

Now the author of this prayer certainly had in mind actual nourishment—the wheaten loaf or *any* food on our tables. Though he asks neither wealth nor poverty, he *does* need his 'daily bread'—which immediately reminds us, of course, of the petition for daily bread in the 'Lord's Prayer'. Moreover, in the same way that the petition 'give us this day our daily bread' can be extended to *any* concrete daily need, bodily or spiritual, so too can 'the food that is needful for me' refer to *any* aspect of daily living in which we call upon God's help and blessings. And, it is for us to *wait* upon His loving care. 'The eyes of all wait upon You, O Lord, and You give them food in due season. You open Your hand and satisfy the desire of every living thing.'[1]

But (lest we forget), whether we call it the 'food we need' or 'our daily bread', when we ask for this we are praying for something even *more* needful. It is something given only in the 'due season' ordained by God alone. We are asking really for the 'daily bread' of His Will for us, whatever that may be. (And God's Will unfolds simply through what *is* each day. . . .) And if this Word sometimes seems sweet in the mouth but bitter when swallowed,[2] let us remember Him whose whole life was nourished by the food unknown to others of doing the Father's will.[3] *He* knew how hard it is to drink this cup.[4] 'O Lord, *thou* knowest, thou *knowest*'. . . .[5] And so, He has given us *the* 'one thing needful',[6] *the* Daily Bread of Communion.

* * *

[1] Psalm 104:27f
[2] Apocalypse 10:9
[3] John 4:32-34
[4] Luke 22:42
[5] Jeremiah 15:15
[6] Luke 10:42

THE FOOD I NEED

'O, feed me with the food I need—the meat
needful for me, Lord! (Give today
my daily bread.)' Ah, good to pray
thus, little children, to repeat
dependence on our Abba's gifts—sweet
nourishment to sustain your way
(pilgrimage) on earth, that you may lay
into your penny barns grain to eat.

Yet, when you farm for Him the food
needful for you, you are asking more
than any laden table, cup flowing
over. Nay . . . you ask that unto you
His Will be done. But, fear not. I bore
a red chalice once—your bread I know.

BREAD FROM HEAVEN
(Wisdom 16:20f)

And He rained down upon them manna to eat,
*   and gave them the grain of heaven.*
Men ate of the bread of angels;
*   He sent them food in abundance. . . .*

You gave Your people the food of angels,
*   and without their toil*
*   You supplied them with food from heaven—*
with bread to eat,
*   providing every pleasure*
*   and suited to every taste.*
For Your sustenance manifested Your sweetness
*   towards your children.*
And the Bread,
*   ministering to the desire of the one who took it,*
*   was changed*
*   to suit everyone's liking.*

* * *

Once again we are concerned with the theme of the Exodus manna. Indeed, the words in the tradition have become so fixed that we have almost identical phrases in two different poetical books of the Bible. Both Wisdom and Psalm 78 speak of God's 'raining' down bread from heaven, giving men the 'food of angels' to eat. It is, of course, a poetic presentation of the historical narrative in Exodus, just as the description of this bread as 'providing every pleasure or sweetness' springs from the record that the manna tasted like honey. We need not dwell long on this imagery because the traditional Exodus symbolism is its best explanation. But, there is a point of comparison—or contrast—with what *we* know to be the true 'bread from heaven'. Instead of the cold rain of 'angels' bread, God sent down the tears (of both pain and joy) of His flesh-warm Son. He needed no miracle, no ministers, no intermediaries in the supernatural order. He needed only that this Son be 'born of a woman',[1] so that this Bread of Himself might be human as the breasts that fed Him and real as the sheaves of wheat He gathered for her.

* * *

[1] Galatians 4:4

BREAD FROM HEAVEN

Heaven opened . . . and He rained grain
upon them, bread of angels—man's meat—
containing all sweetness, manna wheat
white upon the desert. . . . So the saying
of Wisdom—Exodus recalled again,
children in the wilderness, feeding
on the dew fall of flakes, seed
of all future harvests from Yahweh.

Heaven opened—and He came down
Bread Himself, Himself fed of man
(no need for angels . . .)—sweet as breast
milk that suckled Him and field's brown
wheat He touched and kissed to Love-manna—
wilderness in living Grain's caress.

THE BUDDING VINE
(Sirach 24:17-22)

Like a vine I caused loveliness to bud,
    and my blossoms became glorious and abundant fruit.

I am the mother of beautiful love, of reverence,
    of knowledge, and of holy hope.
Being eternal,
    I am therefore given to all my children,
    to those who are named by Him.

Come to me, you who desire me,
    and eat your fill of my produce.
For the remembrance of me is sweeter than honey,
    and my inheritance sweeter than the honeycomb.

Those who eat me will hunger for more,
    and those who drink me will thirst for more.
Whoever obeys me will not be put to shame,
    and those who work with my help
    will not stray.

*   *   *

The 'Wisdom Literature' of the Old Testament derives its name from that trend in the culture of Israel and of the ancient East which led men to ferret out the 'secrets of life' and the *savoir faire* of behaviour in any situation. Pithy sayings, proverbs, psalms, instructions on etiquette, and various forms of the *mashal* or 'parable'—all these reflect the Wisdom stream in Hebrew thought. But, there are other passages in the Old Testament in which Wisdom herself is personified. She is pictured as holding out to man the rich rewards of seeking her and keeping company with her. And one of the loveliest of such passages is that in Sirach in which Wisdom describes her fruits and invites us to partake of them. From eternity God has created her. And she was beside Him—His delight—like a little child when He lay the foundations of the earth.[1] She was given a resting place in the beloved city of Jerusalem, and there she grew tall, grace-full, and verdant as all the trees in the Holy Land.[2] Most marvellous of all, she grew into a vine upon which loveliness and blossoms and fruit ripened. And so, she calls all to taste of her ripeness—which is far sweeter than honey.

But the true fruit of this passage is to be found in the christian interpretation which has been given to it. The 'clue' is found in the verse which is added to some versions of the text: 'I am the *mother* of beautiful love, of reverence, of knowledge, and of holy hope.' This 'mother' can be seen as Mary herself. And though other Old Testament passages in which Wisdom speaks have also been applied to her, this text is special in that this Wisdom—this Mary—is envisaged as giving *birth* to a 'loveliness' far greater than she. Yes, she bore the 'glorious fruit' of Love Himself. And though He first budded from the vine of her, she—and all of us—were then to become part of the true Vine of Him. He the Vine, she the bud, we the branches![3]

And to this 'christian interpretation', we can add our own. We can imagine Mary smiling quietly (was she not but a little child at her Father's side?). Hearing these words applied to her, she knows, nevertheless, that they refer *not* to herself—but to her Son. (For, Mary is she who wishes to be ... only in relation to *Him,* only the silent woman behind the spoken Word....). She knows: He is the Vine, He is the one who calls 'Come to Me!'[4], and He is the sweetness surpassing honey. She knows: had He alone not satisfied her hunger and relieved her thirst?[5] Had He not done this as neither Wisdom nor she could do for us alone? She had tasted His sweetness, eaten His Bread, and known: 'He who eats Me shall live because of Me. ... And because *I* live, you shall live also!'[6]

* * *

[1] Proverbs 8:30
[2] Sirach 24:8-10
[3] John 15:1-6
[4] Matthew 11:28; John 5:40
[5] John 6:35
[6] John 6:57; 14:19

THE BUDDING VINE

... And I, Mary, humble handmaid, smile
that Sirach's words were later hallowed for
my name—that vine-love-liness I caused
to fruit into abundant blossoms, while
my memory (sweeter than the child
of bees—honey) beckons towards my door
(though still hungering and thirsting more,
all those who sup of Me). I smile!

Why? Because such prophecy is true—
not of me (only handmaid) but
of Child I fed ... to feed me! He the Vine,
He the honey lying in Bread food
beyond all hunger, He the Wine cup
unthirsting ... Life first *His*—then mine.

HUNGER
(Lamentations 2:11f; 4:4)

My eyes are spent with weeping;
my soul is in tumult.
My heart is poured out in grief
because of the destruction of the daughter of
my people—
because infants and babes
faint in the streets of the city.

They cry to their mothers,
'Where is bread and wine'? . . .

The tongue of the nurseling
cleaves to the roof of its mouth for thirst.
The children beg for bread,
but no one gives to them.

* * *

Hunger—man has always hungered. He has hungered for so many things . . . and all can be represented in 'bread'. Adam was given the punishment of both needing daily bread and having to toil for it with the sweat of his brow;[1] in the Exodus desert, the people craved the food they had left behind them;[2] the Samaritan woman cried for a living water which would perpetually quench her thirst;[3] the Jews clamoured for an everlasting life-giving bread;[4] and finally,

Jesus Himself knew hunger.[5] Yes, man has hungered for nourishment. From all the manifold biblical images of the enjoyable fruits of the earth to the tiniest vignette of a woman slipping a grain or two of leaven into her wheatmeal dough,[6] man has indeed hungered for nourishment. He has seemed to live *for* 'bread alone'. And this is good . . . for man is man. And the Word Himself became man that He might invite the poor—all of us—to sup with Him in the earthly tent He has pitched in our midst.

But, even having been fed on the fruits of the earth, there is always still a hungering, always a hungering. And it is a hunger unto death—whether it be the death of a body after four score years of eating and drinking, or the death of the spirit after even one moment's unsuccessful search for a deeper nourishment. 'Your fathers ate the manna in the wilderness, and they died.'[7] Ate . . . yet died! Mystery! Yet, no mystery, but the starkly clear reality of life and death given to all seed of mankind. And, we recall, even Wisdom herself—representing the deepest intellectual hungerings of man—cannot satisfy. 'Those who eat me will hunger for *more,* those who drink me will thirst for *more.'*[8] (Even when we apply this text to Mary, she too cannot satisfy our hunger in herself, but only in the Bread of her Son.)

And so, we conclude our Old Testament passages not with the theme of fulness which we have noted in them, but with that of emptiness. We leave with the wail of hunger in our ears—a cry all the more piercingly hopeless because it comes not from men (who are at least able to toil for food), but from children—helpless. We hear the cry of famished babes in the streets of the ruined Jerusalem. They have been recorded by an unknown poet at the time of the siege and Exile whose songs of Lament were ascribed to Jeremiah.

45

But, our choice to conclude with this wail of empty hunger is deliberate. For, the Old Testament itself is necessarily empty and incomplete. It is waiting—'hungering'—for its fulfilment in the New Testament. It is waiting for the New Jerusalem to replace these hollow, famine-struck ruins. It is hungering for *Jesus,* the only Bread that can really satisfy both man's body and spirit. It is the living bread come down from heaven that a man may eat of it and *not* die.[9] If all hungering is a search, it is *He* we really seek. We shall seek Him and we shall find Him when we have searched for Him with *all* our heart.[10] Here is help and Hope for the hungering babes who are really ourselves in our exile. Here is the jar of meal which is never spent.[11] For, 'he who comes to *Me* shall not hunger, and he who believes in *Me* shall never thirst.'[12]

* * *

[1] Genesis 3:19
[2] Exodus 16:3; Numbers 11:4-6
[3] John 4:15
[4] John 6:34
[5] Luke 4:2
[6] Luke 13:20f
[7] John 6:49
[8] Sirach 24:21
[9] John 6:50
[10] Deuteronomy 4:29; Jeremiah 29:10-14
[11] 1 Kings 17:8-16
[12] John 6:35

HUNGER

Lamentations. . . . Seldom do we hear
(more often fear) the mournful wailing
of these death songs, lamenting near
the ruins of Jerusalem, raped
virgin Sion. Here the faint cries
of children, who, bereaved of dried breast,
seek famished for the bread and wine
hungered by their barren mothers. . . . Blessed,
O, blessed the fruitful Womb descended through
that test of exile! Lo, her milk flowed,
fed, and quieted one Child—food
Himself, Bread and Wine! For all know

the (secret) cry of lamentation, cleaving tongue
of hunger-thirst. And all he feeds . . .

pleading, 'Come!'

2. The New Testament

SOMETHING TO EAT
(Mark 5:21-24, 35-43)

And when Jesus had crossed again in the boat to the other side, a great crowd gathered about Him. He was beside the sea. Then came one of the rulers of the synagogue, Jairus by name. And seeing Him, he fell at His feet and besought Him, saying, 'My little daughter is at the point of death. Come and lay Your hands on her, so that she may be well and live.' And Jesus went with him. . . .

While He was still speaking, there came from the ruler's house some who said, 'Your daughter is dead. Why trouble the Teacher any further?' But ignoring what they said, Jesus said to the ruler of the Synagogue, 'Do not fear! Only believe.' And He allowed no one to follow Him except Peter and James and John the brother of James. When they came to the house of the ruler of the synagogue, He saw a tumult. People were weeping and wailing loudly.

And when He had entered, He said to them, 'Why do you create such a tumult and weep? The child is not dead. She is only sleeping.' And they laughed at Him. But, He put them all outside, and took the child's mother and father and those who were with Him, and then went in where the child was. Taking her by the hand, He said to her, 'Talitha cumi.' (This means: 'Little girl, I say to you, arise.') And immediately the girl got up and walked. She was twelve years old. And immediately they were overcome with amazement.

And Jesus strictly charged them that no one should know this, and He told them to give her something to eat.

* * *

The synoptic account of the raising of the daughter of Jairus can be seen as a little 'epiphany' of Jesus, a manifestation of His true self as it is to be revealed through the Resurrection. It is also a testimony to the faith which brings salvation: 'Do not be afraid; only *believe*!' Jairus, wishing that his daughter be *saved* to *live,* is unknowingly asking that Jesus give her eternal life. (And 'eternal life' means not only 'life after death', but also that special quality of 'true, real life' here-and-now which Jesus brings in His very person.)

We can picture the scene: Jesus, accompanied by only the three most intimate of His disciples, enters the chamber of the dead girl and makes the astounding claim that the child is not really dead but only asleep! A seeming impossibility! Whereupon, 'they laughed at Him'—the 'professional mourners laughed scornfully, while the parents of the child probably 'laughed' with a mixture of relief, wild hope, and hopeless tears. They cannot perceive the truth of this enigmatic statement. But, through the eyes of the early Church, which had passed through the transforming power of the Easter experience, Jesus is saying that death is really no more than a 'sleep' from which we awaken in resurrection. For, He is shortly to do for the child exactly what the Father shall do for the Son at His own death upon the Cross, and hence what that Son shall do for all of us. (Indeed, the same Greek words are used in this narrative as in the Resurrection accounts.) Yes, Jesus takes her by the hand, whispering '*Talitha Cumi*' (meaning in Aramaic, 'Get up, little girl' or 'little lamb'!). And, she arises.

But why do we include such a story *here,* among our selection of 'eucharistic' passages? The mother of the child would understand why ... and this is what our poem wishes to express. Simply, the last verse of the account adds the life—like snippet of a certain detail: Jesus asks that the child be given at once 'something to eat'. The grasp of His hands around hers had raised her to new life. And now, His equally tangible hold on reality and His sensitivity to the humanness of Everyday moves Him to this most practical of all concerns that her bodily life be nourished. And so, in our later interpretation, it is not hard to understand (as her mother may have sensed) that Jesus Himself performed this gesture: He slipped a morsel of food into the child's hands, and this Food is the living Bread which sustains her eternal life here-and-now.

* * *

SOMETHING TO EAT

It seemed impossible, though I had read
in the Word, 'Can anything be too
hard for God?' My lamb-daughter—dead—
though my worn breasts had nursed her through
the years delicate with childhood
and she stood on the (still more fragile) sill
of flowering—dead. Yet, the Man
entered: 'Weep not, the child will
live! She is not dead, but only sleeps.'
But I (even I) laughed—how
impossible when a mother keeps
watchful vigil. . . . But I know now.

'*Talitha,* my lamb-child, arise up!'
And she lived . . . because He gave her Bread to sup.

THE CHILDREN'S BREAD
(Mark 7:24-30)

Jesus arose and went away to the region of Tyre and Sidon. And He entered a house, and would not have any one know it. Yet, He could not be hid.

Immediately a woman, whose little daughter was possessed by an unclean spirit, heard of Him and came and fell down at His feet. Now the woman was a Greek, a Syrophoenician by birth. And she begged Him to cast the demon out of her daughter.

And He said to her: 'Let the children first be fed, for it is not right to take the children's bread and throw it to the dogs.' But she answered Him, 'Yes, Lord; yet even the dogs under the table eat the children's crumbs.' And Jesus said to her, 'For this saying you may go your way. The demon has left your daughter.'

And she went home, and found the child lying in bed, and the demon gone.

* * *

But what a strange episode to include in a collection of Communion texts—the story of the Syro-phoenician woman! Not only is the passage not that well-known. But also, when we do read it, we are a trifle embarrassed that Jesus can have spoken in such a manner to anyone, let alone to a woman beseeching His help for her sick child. We must overlook these feelings, though, and try to understand the theological position of this narrative in the gospels. We must consider first of all that the whole story turns about what Jesus tells the woman concerning His mission. She, being a Greek, was not one of the chosen people; and He says that 'the children must first be fed'—that is, He must confine His mission to Israel. Hence, 'it is not right' or fair to grant her request by healing her little daughter, since such an act would be tantamount to giving the 'children's' good bread to mere dogs.

But, the woman's faith in Him, the same faith which had sought Him out to begin with, remains unshaken. And her reply to Him, as heartfelt and sincere as it is clever, wins His praise and His healing. 'O woman, great is your faith! Be it done for you as you desire.'[1] Though He knew that (during His lifetime, at least) He had been 'sent only to the lost sheep of the house of Israel',[2] yet the faith of one small ewe-lamb from another flock[3] overcame all formality. (And we cannot really imagine His having acted otherwise, since Jesus' whole message placed mercy and love above any regulation. . .).

And so, what can this passage possibly hold for our own lives? Everything! In the very humanness of it, everything. For, in us is the woman who cries, so quietly, 'Lord, help me.'[4] In us are the 'dogs', the nobodys, who yet *believe* tenaciously in His power to save (and in His Love which *is* that power). For, is it not because we are men as 'dogs' that God had to become Man as Saviour? And, although we often feel unworthy even to gather the crumbs from under His altar-table, He *always* lifts us up, seats us in the highest places, and feeds us with the finest Bread—of Life.

* * *

[1] Matthew 15:28
[2] Matthew 15:24
[3] John 10:16
[4] Matthew 15:25

THE CHILDREN'S BREAD

'Jesus . . . He who saves . . . You are He
who saves . . . Jesus, Saviour! I (Forgive)
am no one—yet, I know You . . . for I need
You: please, heal my child to live!'
'Woman, would that . . . (Abba, hard this task—
ah, but not *My* will) . . . would that I
were meant to give the child's life you ask.
But other children call. Can it be right
to take their bread for dogs (such as they—
not I—would see you)?' 'Yes, Lord . . . but those
dogs (the no-bodys—myself) disdain
not the crumbs beneath the children's toes. . . .'

'Go, woman, find your child saved.
You have believed—Life, this Bread I gave!'

ONE LOAF ONLY
(Mark 8:14-21)

Now the disciples had forgotten to bring bread, and they had only one loaf with them in the boat.

And Jesus cautioned them, saying, 'Take heed! Beware of the leaven of the Pharisees and the leaven of Herod.' And they discussed it with one another, saying, 'We have no bread.'

And being aware of it, Jesus said to them, 'Why do you discuss the fact that you have no bread? Do you not yet perceive or understand? Are your hearts hardened? Having eyes do you not see? And having ears, do you not hear? Do you not remember? When I broke the five loaves for the five thousand, how many baskets full of broken pieces did you take up?' They said to Him, 'Twelve'. 'And the seven for the four thousand, how many baskets full of broken pieces did you take up?' And they said to Him, 'Seven'.

And Jesus said to them, 'Do you not yet understand?'

* * *

Mark's little vignette of the disciples in the boat with 'only one loaf' culminates that section of his gospel which seems to have a peculiar concentration on the theme of 'bread'. This section contains the account of the *loaves* and fishes which fed the multitude, the story of the Syrophoenician woman with the 'children's *bread*', a second narrative of the

58

feeding of the multitude, and now this reference to a *loaf* in the boat followed by Jesus' enigmatic warning, 'Beware of the *leaven* of the Pharisees'. Moreover, this incident provides the setting for Jesus to voice the piercing grief He felt—a sorrow approaching anger—because His disciples *still* 'did not understand about the loaves, but their hearts were hardened.'[1] Grumbling among themselves about the fact that they had forgotten to bring bread with them in the boat, the disciples incite Jesus to ask a series of eight questions punctuated by a single, poignant refrain: 'Do you *not yet understand*?' Did they not, did they still not perceive what the bread meant—even after His feeding the multitudes in the wilderness? Did they still not understand His loving care for them? Did they still not perceive who He really was? (O, foolish of heart and slow to believe. . . .'[2]

But Mark—*he* has understood, *he* has perceived. For, writing his gospel after Easter, Mark has *believed*. He has come to understand the *real* meaning of the 'miracle' of the loaves and fishes and of every other reference to 'bread' which Jesus may have made. Mark has understood . . . because, in the Eucharistic celebration of the early Church, he has come to know Jesus as the living Bread Himself. And so, it seems that he has included this little 'boat scene' in his gospel at this point because he wishes to express that the bread *is* Jesus. The statement that, although they had 'forgotten to bring bread', yet they had 'only one loaf with them in the boat' is somewhat enigmatic. But Mark has added this because *he* sees who this 'One Loaf' really is.[3] He is the Eucharistic Bread in whom we as many are made one; He is *the* one, the One Thing needful.[4]

* * *

[1] Mark 6:52
[2] Luke 24:25

[3] 1 Corinthians 10:17
[4] Luke 10:42

59

ONE LOAF ONLY

One loaf, only one small
loaf had My disciples on the sea;
and the wave-breakers broke free
against their rowing, bending even tall
manhood into weariness. And all,
hungering, wondering that we
had only one loaf, lamentingly
cried more . . . until a whispered Call

broke silence through the storm. I
was there. And I, their one Loaf—enough.
And you too, upon your Galilee,
your Everyday, take refreshment—mine
is true food! Take Bread brushed
with Wine-love: take, eat, of Me.

DAILY BREAD
(Luke 11:2-4)

And Jesus said to the disciples,

'When you pray, say

Father, hallowed be thy name.
Thy kingdom come.
Give us each day our daily bread (for the morrow);
and forgive us our debts,
for we ourselves forgive everyone who is indebted to us.
And lead us not into temptation.'

* * *

'Give us this day our daily bread. . . .' What can we say about the most familiar 'bread' reference in the Bible for all Christians? What can we add to an understanding of a sentence whose precise nature has baffled theologians throughout the centuries and provoked scholars to write reams of explanations as to its exact meaning? We can say really nothing. And it lies neither in our purpose nor in our ken to enter into the philological and spiritual arguments. It is all the more anomalous in that this dispute concerns the exact meaning of words, the 'daily bread', which are usually repeated so swiftly and unreflectingly by all of us 'daily' that they (not to mention the entire Lord's Prayer) cease to have any meaning at all!

61

And so, let us correct at least that. In our brief look at this prayer here, let us first of all pause long enough to allow just the simple words themselves to fill our spirits. 'Give us this day our daily bread'—what a natural, indeed necessary, request to make of the Father who alone can care for us! For, we are asking not only for actual food. Far more, we are asking for all the necessities of living—and Life itself—for which we are completely dependent on Him. We are asking too (as we noted in our discussion of Proverbs 30:8) that God give us the 'bread' of *whatever* His Will for us may be each day. Indeed, we are really repeating the preceding petition: 'Your will be done on earth as it is in heaven.' But, it is to the central petition of the Lord's Prayer that we turn to really understand what the 'daily bread' means: 'Your Kingdom come'. In asking this, we are asking that all the fulness of God's reign be given to our ordinary, everyday lives here and now.

And, despite appearances, it is really a similar thing that we are asking in the petition for daily bread. The crux (hard crust!) lies in the adjective *epiousion,* a word of uncertain meaning. This is usually translated 'daily' in connection with Luke's version which says 'Give us . . . day-by-day' (as against Matthew's 'today').

But, the more probable meaning of the word is connected with the idea of 'the morrow', so that the petition should be read: 'Give us today (or each day) our bread for tomorrow. . . .' (And it should also be noted that Matthew's verb in Greek implies a single act of giving, whereas Luke's refers to a continuous act—'Keep on giving. . .').

What, then, in this case does the 'morrow's bread' mean but the Food of *the* Tomorrow? The Kingdom is besought to enter our poor lives here and now! No, it is not that the petition ceases to refer to the 'daily bread' of necessities, for it is from these that we must begin. It is rather that, given the *goodness* of this human bread and our hunger for it, the goodness of the homespun fabric of our daily lives, we are also asking that a Heavenly Bread be joined to that. *This* is a more lasting and spiritual food. We are asking that, into the midst of all that we associate with home and a mother's care and hot bread laid upon a wooden table, God the Father might send His own Kingdom's Food. As we wait the final coming of this Kingdom, the form taken by this nourishment is the Bread of Communion. It is wedded to the ordinary food of our daily lives, and in this union we meet Jesus. And so often as we eat this Bread, we do so in memory of Him . . . until He comes.[1]

* * *

[1] 1 Corinthians 11:24, 26

DAILY BREAD

'Our Father, give us bread today,
our daily bread', I have taught you ask
our *Abba*. What means it when you pray
thus? . . . Ah, children, life's task
tires you betimes and you grow weary,
heavy-laden, and your hunger rest,
a hearth fire, Mother wiping tears
from your lone cheek with love blessed
bread—all signs of home. And yet, more
Food, another Home, you hunger for
besides—rest-refreshment I prepare
in our Father's Kingdom. . . . Hence, your prayer:
'Tomorrow's and today's bread be One!'

I answer: in the Wafer, I come.

THE KINGDOM'S FRUIT
(Luke 22:14-18)

And when the hour came, Jesus sat at table, and the apostles were with Him. And He said to them, 'I have earnestly desired to eat this passover with you before I suffer. For I tell you I shall not eat it again until it is fulfilled in the Kingdom of God.'

And He took a cup. And when He had given thanks He said, 'Take this, and divide it among yourselves. For I tell you that from now on I shall not drink of the fruit of the vine until the Kingdom of God comes.'

* * *

Luke's version of the Institution of the Eucharist is the fullest of the synoptic accounts—and a puzzlement as well. Because it seems to contain repetition, even early manuscripts of the gospel differ in their wording. Some give a longer text than others. The 'puzzlement' seems to be occasioned by the reference to another meal before the actual 'Last Supper', a 'paschal meal' which Jesus yearned to share with His disciples. 'I have earnestly desired to eat this Passover with you before I suffer.' It is a yearning which must remain unfulfilled because, He tells us, He shall not eat or drink until the fulfilled Kingdom comes. What does all this mean? In Mark, the words seem more understandable in that they occur *after* the Supper and hence have a purely eschatological significance. But, in actual fact, it is Luke's context which expresses more perfectly the theological import of the sayings. Here, Jesus enacts the Jewish paschal meal to prefigure (and contrast with) the new christian passover which He is about to found in the Eucharist. This, the Last Supper, is to be the 'fulfilment' of the Passover and the 'coming' of the kingdon. And, it is to happen here-and-now—not only for Jesus and His disciples, but for all of us.

Yet, the eschatological or future note remains in the passage. However or wherever we read it, we cannot but sense what Jesus is really saying. He is saying that He is going to die. Yes, though the disciples had not been able to grasp this (or shrank from it) ever since He first told them of the sufferings in store for them,[1] He is here telling them implicitly that He *is* going to die. This, plainly, is why He shall not be having any more meals with them (which is perhaps why, Luke tells us, He not merely 'desired' to eat, but 'earnestly' did so—'desired with desire', the Greek reads). And so, within these sayings, there cannot help being a note of sadness. . . .

Yet, far louder is the hymn of joy! Joy—Because Jesus *knows* that this death is to be the whole secret of Real Life. Though we cannot even begin to fathom the pain of His having to drink the Chalice of His Father's Will, He *knows* the eventual outcome. At a similar moment before His passion, Jesus spoke of the seed that had to die in the earth—but only so that much fruit might come from it.[2] He knew what He was saying: the seed was Himself. And so, His exclamations in this paschal text are filled with Hope— the gladsome hope of sharing meals again with His disciples (now His friends)[3] both in quiet moments before the Ascension and forever afterwards in the Eucharist. The 'fruit of the vine' in the Kingdom was to be His own blood

shed for us ... so that He might rise to Life. If Jesus'
words were set in the Passover rite, they must implicitly
contain the words of the great *Hallel* psalm which was such
an important part of the rite:

> 'I shall not die, but live,
>   and recount the deeds of the Lord.
> The Lord has chastened me sorely,
>   but He has not given me over to death.'[4]

* * *

[1] Matthew 16:21-23; 17:22f; Mark 9:30-32
[2] John 12:24
[3] John 15:15
[4] Psalm 118:18

THE KINGDOM'S FRUIT

Not again shall I drink from
the vine's fruit . . . until I drink anew
in the Kingdom of My Father. You
must hear this Word clearer: death must come
before I eat of grape and wheat again. Some
of you (who shun to watch and pray through
the Dark's last vigil) mourn, 'not true—
dying is far from you, beloved Son!'

And I, too, was anguished to receive
this Chalice—till asking Life's sweet,
vine-blood secret, I have found it, dawn
lit, in . . . death. Yes, like the seed
fruitful through its ground dying. . . . O, meet
Life in me through death. Be reborn!

THE ROAD TO EMMAUS
(Luke 24:13-35)

That very day, two of Jesus' followers were going to a village named Emmaus, about seven miles from Jerusalem. They were talking with each other about all these things that had happened. While they were talking and discussing together, Jesus Himself drew near and went with them. But their eyes were kept from recognizing Him. And He said to them, 'What is this conversation which you are holding with each other as you walk?' And they stood still, looking sad.

Then one of them, Cleopas by name, answered Him. 'Are you the only visitor in Jerusalem who does not know the things that have happened there in these days?' And He said to them, 'What things?' And they said to Him, 'Concerning Jesus of Nazareth, who was a prophet mighty in deed and word before God and all the people, and how our chief priests and rulers delivered Him up to be condemned to death, and crucified Him. But we had hoped that He was the one to redeem Israel! Yes, and besides all this, it is now the third day since this happened. Moreover, some women in our company amazed us. They were at the tomb early in the morning and did not find His body. And they came back saying that they had even seen a vision of angels, who said that He was alive. Some of those who were with us went to the tomb, and found it just as the women had said. But Him they did not see.'

And He said to them, 'O foolish men, and slow of heart to believe all that the prophets have spoken! Was it not

69

necessary that the Christ should suffer these things and enter into His glory?' And beginning with Moses and all the prophets, He interpreted to them in all the scriptures the things concerning Himself.

So they drew near to the village to which they were going. He appeared to be going further, but they constrained Him, saying: 'Stay with us, for it is toward evening and the day is now far spent.' So He went in to stay with them. When He was at table with them, He took the bread and blessed, and broke it, and gave it to them. And their eyes were opened and they recognized Him. And He vanished out of their sight.

They said to each other, 'Did not our hearts burn within us while He talked to us on the road, while He opened to us the Scriptures?' And they rose that same hour and returned to Jerusalem. And they found the eleven gathered together and those who were with them, who said, 'The Lord has risen indeed, and has appeared to Simon!'

Then they told what had happened on the road, and how He was known to them in the breaking of the bread.

* * *

Of all the gospel narratives which afford us glimpses into the life of Jesus, and of all His own words through which we come to know Him as a person, there is somehow none more revealing than this: the story of what happened on the road to Emmaus. It *is* a *story,* and we must realize this. Luke alone among the evangelists relates this episode, and he does so with all the literary art of a *raconteur*. Moreover, it is helpful to realize that it belongs among the 'post-resurrection' narratives of the gospels. As such, the factual material underlying the episode has necessarily been interpreted through the eyes of faith. What actually happened is colored (though not distorted) by the light which Easter shed upon the disciples' understanding of *who* this Jesus *really* was all along. This results in a certain 'tension' in the narrative, something which is brought out clearly by the words of Cleopas to the mysterious Companion who accosted them. He asks Him if He had not heard about the sad happenings in recent days, about the way in which a mighty (and O, so gentle!) prophet named 'Jesus of Nazareth' had actually been crucified? Had He not experienced and heard about the bitter disappointment brought about by this shameful death? They had *hoped* He was the one to *save* Israel. . . . But what, what Hope had they now? And, of course, the 'mysterious stranger' to whom Cleopas was speaking these words was *Himself* this Hope, the living *Saviour*!

The 'tension' in the story is resolved through their recognition of this Jesus. And, yes, this His self-revelation takes place through the 'breaking of the bread'. Now, it need not necessarily be that Luke has in mind here a direct reference to the Eucharist. It could be that the two disciples came to know who this Man really was just through His spending the evening with them and their sharing an ordinary meal with Him as they had so often during His lifetime. But, the facts all suggest that Luke has written this story with an intentional reference to the 'Lord's Supper' already being celebrated in the early christian Church of his day. For, it *is* a post-resurrection narrative dealing with an apparition of Jesus; it includes the liturgical eucharistic formula of taking, blessing, breaking, and giving bread; and it is at *this* moment that Jesus reveals Himself and then vanishes.

However, there is a simpler way in which we can know what this narrative really means. For, how often, in lonely twilights, have we sensed the presence of Another at our sides along our roadways. How often have we felt something burning with love and joy and peace in our hearts as He speaks God's word to us—as if He Himself were that Word. And, we do not want Him to go. We want Him to come and dwell within our everyday lives—our very home and hearth—a Friend for our loneliness. 'Stay with us, for it is toward evening, and the day is now far spent.' And, by the simplest of gestures, by sharing bread at an old wooden table by the light of the fire flames, we feel that flushed glow which is the certainty of who He is: Love. It is the Bread—warm and alive—that tells us: 'I will not leave you alone. I will come to you and make My home within you.'[1] And if our yearning abides in the continuous prayer of '*Stay* with us!', that prayer is answered: 'Lo, I *am* with you *always*. . .'[2]

* * *

[1] John 14:18, 23
[2] Matthew 28:20

THE ROAD TO EMMAUS

Emmaus . . . when we met a lost (we thought)
Friend (and more—Beloved) on the way
weary from the City. . . . Just that day,
on Golgotha, we had seen a cross
empty . . . but for memory of a lost
Companion. And we whispered, just to say
the shame in it—that he, who could have saved
Israel, had died. . . . But then, accosting

us suddenly, One so child-
like (yet a Man—and more) he had not heard
these happenings. And so, we told . . . and bade
Him stay the late evening. Lo! For while
at table, Bread He broke, and burned His Word
into our hearts—Beloved. He *had* saved!

THE GOOD WINE
(John 2:1-11)

On the third day, there was a marriage at Cana in Galilee, and the mother of Jesus was there. Jesus also was invited to the marriage, with His disciples. When the wine failed, the mother of Jesus said to Him, 'They have no wine.' And Jesus said to her, 'O woman, what have you to do with Me? My hour has not yet come.' His mother said to the servants, 'Do whatever He tells you.'

Now six stone jars were standing there, for the Jewish rites of purification, each holding twenty or thirty gallons. Jesus said to them, 'Fill the jars with water.' And they filled them to the brim. He said to them, 'Now draw some out, and take it to the steward of the feast.' So they took it.

When the steward of the feast tasted the water now become wine, and did not know where it came from (though the servants who had drawn the water knew), the steward of the feast called the bridegroom and said to him: 'Every man serves the good wine first. And when men have drunk freely, then he serves the poor wine. But you have kept the good wine until now.'

This, the first of His signs, Jesus did at Cana in Galilee, and manifested His glory. And His disciples believed in Him.

* * *

Cana—how much we have heard about Cana, where Jesus worked the 'first of the signs' in His public ministry. Even the very image of turning water into wine has become all but proverbial. And, how much has been written about this 'miracle—not only about the way in which it 'manifested' Jesus' glory, but even more about the Mother of Jesus as she is here introduced in John's gospel. And, we have heard most of all about the differing interpretations of her Son's addressing her here simply as 'Woman', just as He was to do beneath the Cross.[1] In keeping with our whole approach, we shall not look at the complex implications of the passage. Rather, we shall be simple as 'little children' and look at it in a human way. For Mary, the 'woman' who is the center of the whole episode (precisely because she reveals her Son as *the* center), is but a child herself.

We can imagine realistically the circumstances: an ordinary wedding-feast, but an out-of-the-ordinary occasion in the humble lives of the villagers and hence a time for rejoicing. This rejoicing was so whole-hearted that naturally the wine ran out. And Mary, being woman and exquisitely sensitive, felt keenly for the embarrassment of the host and her fellow guests and wanted to help. And so, she turned to the one whom she most loved and trusted: her Son. She did this *not* because she expected a 'miracle' or knew *what* He was going to do, but only because she *believed* in His power to help. She knew she needed only to inform Him about the situation: 'they have no wine'. She knew she needed only to inform the servants to do *whatever* He told them. Mary did not ask when or how. She simply had complete confidence that He would take care of the situation. And her confidence enabled Him to 'change water into wine'.

And, there is more. The water was stored in stone jars (resembling the smaller jar which Mary must have carried on her head each day from the Nazareth well). And these stone vessels could represent the frame of our own 'everyday', with all the ordinary happenings which God sends to us represented by the 'water' inside. (We must not fear to fill our jars brim-ful with His will.) But, touched by the faith in Mary's heart and the love in Jesus' hands, this 'water' becomes transformed into something sweeter and richer in meaning. It becomes the 'good wine'—the Blood-Wine of communion—'kept until now' just for us, the 'servants' who know the secret. We are given to drink it as we follow Jesus in His Kingdom on earth, that we might have a foretaste of His own Marriage Supper in the Kingdom to come.[2]

* * *

[1] John 19:26
[2] Apocalypse 19:9

THE GOOD WINE

Cana, Cana . . . means . . . Mary, she
(and each) who has believed. For Cana meant
the ordinary happened at a feast
of marriage: good gladness spent
the wine. . . . And Mary, sword-sensitive
as mother to her friends, sought the One,
her Son and most beloved Friend, to give
help (how, it did not matter) from
God's own Hand into this home
of humble everyday. Nothing asking,
nothing knowing, only trusting growing
seeds of her believing, Mary passed

God's *fiat* to a stone flask—Faith's sign
our water-nothingness becomes His Blood Wine.

THE FIVE BARLEY LOAVES
(John 6:4-14)

Now the Passover, the feast of the Jews, was at hand. Lifting up His eyes, then, and seeing that a multitude was coming to Him, Jesus said to Philip: 'How are we to buy bread, so that these people may eat?' This He said to test him, for He himself knew what He would do. Philip answered Him, 'Two hundred denarii would not buy enough bread for each of them to get a little' (a denarius was a day's wage).

One of His disciples, Andrew (Simon Peter's brother), said to Him: 'There is a lad here who has five barley loaves and two fish. But what are they among so many?' Jesus said, 'Make the people sit down.' Now there was much grass in the place. So the men sat down, in number about five thousand.

Jesus then took the loaves. And when He had given thanks, He distributed them to those who were seated. So also the fish, as much as they wanted. And when they had eaten their fill, He told His disciples: 'Gather up the fragments left over, that nothing may be lost.' So they gathered them up and filled twelve baskets with fragments from the five barley loaves, left by those who had eaten.

When the people saw the sign which He had done, they said, 'This is indeed the prophet who is to come into the world!'

* * *

We are all familiar, we think, with the 'Miracle of the Loaves and Fishes' or the 'Feeding of the Multitude' in the gospels. Although the accounts differ and although Jesus may have performed such a 'miracle' on two occasions, it is the *one* and only episode which is repeated almost verbatim in all four gospels. In fact, the whole of what happened can best be glimpsed from piecing together the differing accounts. We could have chosen any of the four to include here, but we have chosen John's narrative because his is the prelude for his 'Bread of Life' discourse. (Also, his is the only one which gives the delightful detail of the 'lad with five barley loaves and two fish'.) If our reflections upon the events in the story itself are brief, this is because they are so well-known to us. A hungry multitude is gathered in a 'lonely place apart'[1] to listen to Jesus teaching; He bids them to sit down upon the green grass; and He distributes to them an abundance of bread out of the mere handful of loaves—such an abundance that there were 'leftovers'!

Another reason for our brevity here is that the various theological interpretations of the passage are so manifold. Because of the scene of a feeding in the wilderness, the association with the Exodus 'manna miracle' is most obvious. Closely connected to this is the idea of 'messianic rest' suggested by Jesus' asking the people to sit down upon the grassy slope. (These could remind us of the 'green pastures' in the 'Shepherd Psalm'.) This same theme is also suggested by the Marcan report that Jesus was moved by 'compassion for them because they were like sheep without a shepherd.[2] The messianic banquet, which was anticipated by the Qumran community, is suggested by the way in which the people 'sat down by companies'.[3]

Of course, the most obvious allusion of all is to the Eucharist. The very fact that all four gospels contain this narrative and use the customary 'eucharistic formula' over the bread (with certain variations) confirms this. Also, the point is made that, where the 'fish' may appear in the story, they seem to be an 'afterthought'. Or, at least their importance has been minimized. And finally, the distribution and gathering up of the loaves by the disciples may indicate liturgical practice in the early Church. (There is also a possible significance to the fact that the grass, Mark tells us, was *green*! Connected with John's reference to the coming Passover, this may mean that the springride setting of the 'miracle' symbolizes the christian Passover—Easter with its eucharistic feast.)

But whatever may have actually happened and whatever interpretation the evangelists later gave to the event, we can perceive its searching meaningfulness for us here and now. We are struck by its poignant portrait of Jesus Himself and His deepest love for us. For, in John's gospel, it is *Jesus* who distributes the loaves—not the disciples. And, later on, it is Jesus too who points out the whole kernel of the event. He is grieved because the people have seen it afterwards *only* as a 'miracle' providing material bread for their hunger (and they would still be hungry again). They have not perceived that it was a sign of something far greater which—Who—would forever satisfy their deeper hunger. In Mark, as we have seen, Jesus grieves because the people did not yet understand what happened and the disciples could not perceive. 'Having eyes do you not see? And having ears, do you not hear? And do you not remember? When I broke the five loaves for the five thousand, how many baskets full of broken pieces did you take up?'[4] Jesus yearns for them to labor not for the 'food that perishes, but for the food that endures to eternal life.'[5]

Jesus knew all too well the bitter, sorrowful truth: the people were flocking to Him not because they saw (that is, understood) the sign, but because they ate their fill of the loaves.[6] In John, 'signs' are not the marvels and wonders which the people often expected—and were criticized for doing so.[7] Rather, they are real events and words in Jesus' life which reveal who He *is*—His true person—for those who have eyes to see. They are a silent call for the most perfect kind of seeing: Believing. The Hebrews once murmured, 'But how *can* God spread a table in the wilderness?'[8] In the same way, the disciples here asked, 'But how *can* such a small bit of bread *possibly* feed so many?' The answer is that we are not meant to ask ... because, in all our desert places, Jesus always feeds us where it would seem impossible. We eat 'as much as we want', and we are satisfied. For, 'all things are possible to him who *believes*!'[9] —yes, even Bread multiplied.

* * *

[1] Mark 6:31, 35
[2] Mark 6:34
[3] Mark 6:39
[4] Mark 8:19f
[5] John 6:27
[6] John 6:26
[7] Matthew 16:4
[8] Psalm 78:19
[9] Mark 9:23

THE FIVE BARLEY LOAVES

Still, still do you not yet
understand, not yet perceive,
not yet accept (so slow believing)
what happened then when I met
the child with five loaves . . . and fed
the multitude over grass green
with Passover? Surely you have seen
(miracle?) and in your hearts kept
pondering this saying-sight. . . . But

hard hearts if still you do not grasp
not the happening, but more—the sign
behind—that to this lone place, shut
from nourishment, bereft of hope, past
love, *I* came . . . and quickened . . . Life.

THE BREAD OF LIFE
(John 6:48-58)

'I AM THE BREAD OF LIFE.'

'Your fathers ate the manna in the wilderness, and they died. This is the bread which comes down from heaven, that a man may eat of it and not die. I am the living bread which came down from heaven. If any one eats of this bread, he will live forever. And the bread which I shall give for the life of the world is My flesh.'

The Jews then disputed among themselves, saying, 'How can this Man give us His flesh to eat?' So Jesus said to them, 'Truly, truly, unless you eat the flesh of the Son of man and drink His blood, you have no life in you. He who eats My flesh and drinks My blood has eternal life, and I will raise him up at the last day. For My flesh is real food, and My blood is real drink.

'He who eats My flesh and drinks My blood abides in Me, and I in him. As the living Father sent Me and I live because of the Father, so he who eats Me will live because of Me. This is the bread which came down from heaven, not such as the fathers ate and died. He who eats this bread will live for ever.'

* * *

'I am the Bread of Life.' Jesus Himself is the life-giving Bread. This is the vibrant well-spring of the entire eucharistic reality. This is the Wheat with which our daily bread is made. If the synoptic evangelists and Paul give us the general framework of the Eucharist and its formal beginnings, it is John who fills—and transcends—that frame with the living Person standing behind it all. For, the entire latter part of Chapter 6 in his gospel, usually known as the 'Bread of Life' discourse, is John's equivalent to the synoptic account of the Last Supper. It represents his own mature meditation upon that Supper in the light of his own participation in partaking of the Bread and the Wine after his Lord's death. When the synoptics record simply the words of the tradition, John speaks from the intimate communion he knew with Jesus as he grasped more and more the meaning of the Resurrection. His words are truly 'spirit and life'. And if John's vision has been compared with that of an eagle in later christian symbolism, it all began because he had been the 'beloved disciple' nesting as a tiny sparrow against the heart beating in Jesus' breast.

Form criticism has carefully tried to discern the manner in which John wrote this discourse. It has tried to distinguish among Jesus' original words, John's meditation on them, and the addenda of later 'editorial hands'. But, in the end, all this is immaterial because the message is clearly the very core of what Jesus intended the Eucharist to be. The message is simply this: *Life*. This Bread is Life, and he who eats it shall *live*. It is a teaching which is in keeping with the whole of John's gospel, because the whole is concerned precisely with the 'eternal life' which Jesus gives us here-and-now in Himself. (This teaching is sometimes known as 'realized eschatology'). When Jesus says here, 'I AM the Bread of Life', it is equivalent to all the other 'I AM'S' in John's gospel: 'I AM . . . the Door, the Good Shepherd, the true Vine, the Light of the World, the Way and the Truth, the Resurrection. . .'. Jesus names these things because *He* is the reality behind them all. He is all things because He is, simply, Life.[1] And when He repeats throughout the gospel that He has come to give us 'eternal life', this does not mean merely 'life after death'. It is that special dimension to life here-and-now which His coming has given to the world, and which is awakened in those who really know Him.[2] It is that 'life in more abundance' which each of us experiences personally through His presence within us.[3]And because this 'Bread' is not just a mere symbol but something we can hold in our hands and taste with our lips and swallow into our very flesh, it is somehow the most meaningful of all John's life-giving designations for Jesus.

It is this reality of *life,* of 'communion' with Jesus by *living* or 'abiding' in Him always, that must guide our reflections in these pages. We cannot even begin to look at every verse in the discourse. Besides, one verse supports and amplifies another, so that to grasp even one is to grasp the whole. Above all, no words about the discourse could clarify what is here so explicitly (and starkly as well). Hence, we shall select only four verses to illustrate. But, behind each, the *context* of the whole must be borne in mind: the chapter begins with the 'multiplication of the loaves' followed by the episode of the storm on the sea. When Jesus assures the disciples there, 'It is I: do not be afraid!',[4] He is revealing the same thing as He is shortly to say about this bread: 'It is *I.*' The discourse itself follows upon Jesus' disappointment that the Jews did not grasp the *true* import of the miracle of the loaves. He subsequently contrasts the manna of the Exodus with the bread *He* gives. Their request, 'Lord, give us this bread always!', stirs the teaching which then follows.

The verse occupying our first illustration is usually

interpreted as the beginning of John's explicit reference to the Eucharist. Heretofore, in speaking of the 'living bread', Jesus was most likely referring to His teaching, to His saving words and person in general. But, henceforth He speaks of the Bread as the body He is to give through His sacrificial death: 'The bread which I shall give for the life of the world is My *flesh.*' These words are thought to be the equivalent of the synoptic 'This is My Body'. (In fact, scholars who are familiar with the Aramaic which Jesus spoke conclude that John preserves the original word—which is unknown to us anyway—more closely than the other evangelists by using the term 'flesh' rather than 'body'.) And, the force of the verse lies in the reason for which Jesus gives this flesh: 'for the *life* of the world.' This means that He is giving eternal life to each of us here and now. For John, the beloved disciple, had come to know: there could be no death for even the tiniest, fallen sparrow because the heavenly Father feeds him with the living Bread of His Son.[5]

* * *

[1] John 14:6
[2] John 17:2f
[3] John 10:10
[4] John 6:20
[5] Luke 12:4-7, 22-24

FOR YOUR LIFE: MY FLESH

'Death, O Love, death—the window pane
swept cold with autumn rain . . . and I
listen bravely through the night sky—
bell tolling musicless the name
death. And I, waiting, know the same
dull throbbing—though, being only child,
ask no miracle . . . but only, why
fell my sparrow when the bell came?'

'Come to Me, my little one! The Son
has risen (healing in My wings). He knows,
my Abba-Father, of your sparrow, yes—
for I, cross-fallen once, come
to give you Life. Through the dawn, lo,
my Song raised strong beyond death.'

* * *

If Jesus has said that He is giving His flesh for the *life* of the
world, and if He has repeated that He is the bread that gives
Life, it follows that without this food there can be no life.
'Unless we eat His flesh and drink His blood, we have no
life within us.' As happened to the Hebrews after eating the
manna in the desert, and as happens to anyone who feeds
on the bread of mortals, we would die. Die. . . . *unless* you
eat'. . . . It *is* a 'hard saying'.[1] It is offensive. Jesus' entire
command to eat His flesh and drink His blood is a 'hard
saying', and it proved so offensive that 'many of His disciples

drew back and no longer went with Him.'² But, this hardness is softened and sweetened if we can grasp what Jesus was really saying. For, He spoke the 'truth that makes us free.'³

A physical body will die without nourishment. And so, the daily way of man is one long toil for daily bread, and he eats this in order that he may continue to live. But, mankind is created with the Spirit of God within him that he may live a deeper life⁴—a life whose meaning and end is not upon this earth at all. It is a life equally as real, and so it requires real nourishment. Jesus gives us, now and forever after, this larger life—'eternal life'. *He* is this Life. Knowing that it must be nourished, He gives us food to sustain it—'living bread'. *He* is this Bread. We remain creatures of flesh-and-blood; we still die. Even though we eat the bread of our toil and the Communion Bread wafer itself as well, we bodily die. Yet, because the life which Jesus gives us is God's own life,⁵ we do *not* die. We live! 'He who believes in Me, though he die, yet shall he live.'⁶ And because that life is nourished here-and-now with the Flesh and Blood of God Himself, we do not ever really die spiritually because our life on earth is fed with this food from above. 'And whoever lives and believes in Me shall never die.'⁷ The crux is: '*Do* you *believe* this?'

For, it is Believing—believing alone—which can overcome the 'hard saying' of the Eucharist. The disciples who stayed with Jesus believed and thus came to know one thing. They realized that they had nowhere else to go but to *Him,* and *His* words alone (however hard and impossible and offensive they might be) could give Life.⁸ John knew more fully than any of them, perhaps. For, he tells us, he wrote down all these things in this gospel—including the words on the Bread of Jesus' flesh—that we might learn to *believe* in Him and through our *Believing* have Life in His name.⁹

* * *

[1] John 6:60
[2] John 6:66
[3] John 8:32
[4] Genesis 2:7; Ezekiel 37:14
[5] John 5:21, 26; John 6:57
[6] John 11:25
[7] John 11:26
[8] John 6:68f
[9] John 20:31

UNLESS YOU EAT . . . .

No life—no, you cannot live
unless . . . you eat My flesh and drink My blood.
Do you fear My word—as if I give
death's sentence heart (you said it was
a hard saying. . .)? Ah, I give heart
to *life* within you . . . for that Life I am!
Can incarnate body be apart
from nourishment, food-drink? And can
(because apart from Me you are not)
your very frame and sinews be sustained
without partaking of My Body—hot
flesh bread and blood wine? Plain—

no Life unless. . . . But lo, no death
if, feeding on Me, you are breathing My Breath!

* * *

We are a people forever seeking 'reality', forever seeking
ultimates. We want to handle what is real and abiding in
life. (This is reflected even by the way in which many of us
use the word 'really' with almost every breath!) For some,
reality becomes most immediate in material objects and
possessions or the means whereby to keep on procuring
them. For others, it signifies all the circumstances of one's
life. (And if that life happens to know bitter hardship and
trial, 'reality' can bear a sorrowful connotation too.)
Reality can be sought in philosophical concepts or abstract

theories in the realm of 'knowledge'. It can be sought in 'spiritual aspirations'. And, most perfectly of all, man seeks it in other persons—in the bond of *love*. This is why 'reality' is to be found . . . in God.

And this is why Jesus has described His flesh as 'real' or 'true' food, His blood as 'real' or 'true' drink. By this, He means that, because they are given us in the tangible form of bread and wine, they are actual food and drink which can nourish our bodies. But, He means far more besides. For, whether it be in earthly food or material things or any other objective in our 'hunger' for 'reality', there is no food which can satisfy our hunger as can His food. There is no thing as 'real' as He is real. The marvel of marvels is this: that this ultimate, infinite truth and reality is all contained in something as small and fragile as a wafer of Bread.

* * *

REAL FOOD, REAL DRINK

Food fathers life. Who of man
survives without it or can consecrate
his hands to work's art, to God's plan
his heart? Hence, in faith, his eyes wait
on Providence to give him meat in due
season—satisfying his need with bread,
wine (to gladden), all good harvest fruit—
strong, succulent. . . . And man is fed.
Yes, food fathers life—and while
growth nourishing, it mothers. . . . So,
Jesus too must have meant Life
by His Body-Blood our food—no

ordinary Bread-Wine, but Life Real—
eternal—born of this fragile wafer meal.

*   *   *

'Live! He who eats this bread will *live*!' The whole of John's
gospel, the whole of his eucharistic teaching is this: Life.
The 'bread discourse' began with a contrast between the
manna which the forefathers of Israel ate only to die, and
the true bread from heaven which God gave so that the new
Israel might live. It ends with the same contrast. For us,
who are raised in the Easter faith, the thought of 'life out
of death' is almost a commonplace. (Indeed, perhaps it is
such because we grasp so little of its true import.) But,
though we *are* meant to rejoice in this Easter victory of life

and let its triumphant light swell our lives with hope, let us not take too lightly what lay behind this victory over death. Let us not forget that One Man first had to die, *had* to die upon a Cross.

And so, whereas it is helpful to discern the theme of 'Life' in Jesus' teaching, in John's interpretation of it, and in this eucharistic passage, we must seek the origin of such a theme and give it a living body. It could not have been a mere immaterial ideal. It must have sprung from a real encounter between life and death in man's experience. It *did* spring from the meeting of one Man's life with death—and Beyond: Jesus. Yes: His whole ministry was a 'call to life' and an active sign that Life had been given to us in His person. But, the reason He could speak His words so forcefully was that, all the time, He knew what it was like to have Death awaiting Him. He knew all of Love's sensitivity to the world's sorrow: 'Jesus wept.'[1]

This, perhaps, is why His eucharistic gift is so profoundly real. Because of His own passion, it is almost passionate. 'He who eats My flesh and drinks My blood abides —*lives*—in Me, and I in Him. . . . He who eats Me shall *live* because of Me, shall live on!' These are the cries of One who had to accept death—total annihilation—before He spoke them. They are the affirmations of One who could only *believe* through all His humanness, just as we must believe, that death is *not* this total end. He believed because He knew His Father's unfailing love for us. John may not give us the precise 'eucharistic words' of the Last Supper. But, he does give us other words which Jesus spoke on that occasion, the 'Farewell Discourse', which make that Eucharist alive. 'As the Father has loved Me, so have I loved you. Abide—Live—in My Love.'[2]

We are so human. Sometimes we do not recognize Jesus. Sometimes it is hard to see Him. We say, with the man born blind, 'But who *is* this Jesus that I may believe in Him?'[3] Knowing our humanness, He gives us the one sure way of always being able to see and touch Him: the Bread of Life. 'You have seen Him, and it is He who speaks to you—speaks by living in this Bread!' It remains for us but to say, 'LORD, I BELIEVE.'

* * *

[1] John 11:35
[2] John 15:9
[3] John 9:36-38; John 4:26

LIVE!

Only one way, only one
way to learn what means this Bread I give—
death. Yes. A hard saying, come
too stark upon your hope clothed to live,
too near to shadows you would rather leave
dark. Ah, do not fear. Take,
took at death, hold it close, receive
into your hands its rough texture, breaking
fear into your hearts. . . . Awake! Turn,
then, take, touch, and warm My white
Bread wafer! Break, eat, learn
of hearts led beyond fear's night;

breathe the last . . . only one way—death—
to grasp . . . My hand then in yours with Bread, new breath!

THE TRUE VINE
(John 15:1-11)

'I AM THE TRUE VINE, and My Father is the vinedresser. Every branch of Mine that bears no fruit He takes away, and every branch that does bear fruit He prunes—so that it may bear more fruit. You are already made clean by the word which I have spoken to you.

'Abide in Me, and I in you.

'As the branch cannot bear fruit by itself unless it abides in the vine, neither can you unless you abide in Me. I am the vine, you are the branches. He who abides in Me, and I in him, he it is that bears much fruit, for apart from Me you can do nothing.

'If a man does not abide in Me, he is cast forth as a branch and withers. And the branches are gathered, thrown into the fire, and burned. If you abide in Me, and My words abide in you, ask whatever you will, and it shall be done for you. By this My Father is glorified, that you bear much fruit, and so prove to be My disciples.

'As the Father has loved Me, so have I loved you. Abide in My love. If you keep My commandments, you will abide in My love—just as I have kept My Father's commandments and abide in His love. These things I have spoken to you, so that My Joy may be in you and your Joy may be full.'

* * *

'Abide in My Love, that My Joy may be in you and your joy may be full!' The allegory of the Vine could well be called the living root of John's gospel. It is the living fruit of Jesus' own love and joy. If it seems profound, this is because it seems so simple—so simple that Jesus sought an allegory as the means by which to explain the deepest truth. It is as He tells it, and He wishes us to picture just that: a stem, branches which have no life at all unless they are part of that stem, and fruit which can never come upon those branches unless they remain in the whole Vine as their only source of nourishment. And, He wants us to picture with equal realism the 'husbandman' who prunes those branches, cutting them way back to the vine-stem. In this way, what has already produced fruit will be enabled to produce more. (And, let us not forget that the Vine suffers as much as the branches in the pruning—Jesus, no less than ourselves, has had to submit to the Shears of God's husbandry. . . .) The image, drawn from the most fundamental processes in plant life, is clear. And, if we have really grasped *this,* we do not need to go further into 'deeper meanings.' For, Jesus uses this image in the first place precisely because, of itself, it already implicitly contains the meaning He intends by it.

But, it may be helpful to say a bit more about it because it is more than merely an image: it is reality, 'I am the *true* Vine'—the *true* Vine, Jesus says. In other words, all that we know of stems and branches and fruits in the natural world is *less* real than the Vine *He* is and the branches *we* are! He is also the 'true vine' as distinct from the 'false' Israel who, throughout the Old Testament, was chosen to be God's own vine—but proved unfaithful. Isaiah's 'Song of the Beloved and His Vineyard' tells of how Yahweh (the Beloved) carefully cultivated and prepared His choicest 'pleasant planting', Israel, to produce wine. But, when He looked for her yield, it was only wild grapes.[1] But Jesus—Jesus is the true vineyard, the only *real* vine.

In describing Himself in this way, Jesus has also chosen a very apt image because of the manifold references throughout the entire Bible to grapes, wine ('the blood of the grape'), and vineyards. It is, of course, most appropriate of all in terms of the Eucharist. He fulfills the Vine reality perfectly in His having given us His own blood in the form of Wine. Whenever we drink this cup, we know that the 'fruit of the earth and work of human hands' contained in this Wine has not only all come from Him, but *is* Himself. We are the branches, and the grapes that we bear return to their Giver—the Vine—through His Wine!

But . . . our words only cloud the clear mystery. He has asked us simply to 'abide', to rest, in Him. And if the whole allegory is rooted in the fact that 'apart from Me you can do *nothing*', we can never really be apart from Him. The branch *is* a part of the Vine. And, 'I can do *all* things in Him who strengthens me.'[2]

* * *

[1] Isaiah 5:1-7
[2] Philippians 4:13

THE TRUE VINE

Could you but know, could you but know, the thing
most hidden from you (for—man—alone
you think to stand. . .). O, anew I sing
a love-song of God's Vineyard—now grown
into the true Vine! Beloveds, I
am He . . . and you the branches bound in me
by one blood-love. Rest—abide—
in Me: apart from me, you can do or be
nothing. But . . . just abide: apart
you never are. I the Vine, and you
the branches—do not fear! Let not your heart
be troubled when your leaves suffer, pruned:

grapes—Wine-fruit—you bear, poured warm
again into the Vine-blood where you were born.

THE CROSS
(John 19:30, 34f)

When Jesus had received the vinegar, He said, 'It is finished.' And He bowed His head and gave up His spirit. . . .

But one of the soldiers pierced His side with a spear, and at once there came out blood and water.

He who saw it has borne witness—his testimony is true. And he knows that he tells the truth—that you also may believe.

* * *

In every passage we have selected thus far in both Testaments, there has been some explicit mention of bread or wine, 'fruits of the earth and work of human hands'. Whether a direct reference to the Eucharist or merely an association, this bread and wine have been tangible foods which we can see with our eyes and touch with our hands. Jesus has given us this Sacrament of 'Communion' in such a perceptible form because, as Man Himself, He knows our humanness. . . .

But, none of the 'eucharistic texts' in the Bible, no participation in the Lord's Supper, and no celebration of Mass can have any meaning without *the* One Thing which really stands behind this Bread and Wine. This 'one thing' is the ultimate of both the tangible and the intangible; it is the ultimate experience of Jesus as both Man and God. This 'one thing' is the true meaning of the Incarnation. It is the secret of His flesh living on in the Bread and His blood in the Wine. It is the means whereby we who eat this Flesh and drink this Blood abide in Him and receive eternal life. And it is the sign of Christianity. We can mention it here only briefly, for it is really beyond words (and holds the hardest of all 'hard sayings'). But without it, we would not be. It is . . . The Cross.

The Cross! Yes, the sign in all our homes and churches, the mark inscribed on anything since the first days of Christianity—from underground stones to forest trees to steeples in the sky and even to pendants around our necks. Indeed, it goes back even further—to the moment of Golgotha itself! We have mentioned the Cross indirectly in all our passages in some way or another. We have accepted it and presupposed it—even taken it for granted—in our stressing the theme of Life's triumph over death in the symbol of the Living Bread. But, we must pause here to look at it directly. For, what does it *really* mean, this Cross? It has a greater significance than death, or even life through death.

It means . . . sacrifice, Sacrifice! It means that one Man—God—*gave* Himself up to die . . . for *us*. The Cross: it is this which is implicit in all the titles later given to Jesus: Saviour, Redeemer, Messiah, Son of Man, Lord. It is this which was the passionately driving power behind the apostleship of Paul, who gloried in nothing but the 'cross of Jesus Christ'[1] and claimed to know and preach nothing but Christ crucified. And with Him, Paul too had been crucified.[2] Finally, it is this sacrifice which is the heart of the Mass, as is made clear by the very words of 'institution': This is My Body which is to be *given* for you.' We have stressed that Jesus says He is giving His flesh for the *Life* of the world. But, we must stress equally that it *is* a *Giving*—through His death.

We could have chosen a portion of any of the gospels' crucifixion narratives to make us aware of the Eucharist as a sacrifice. However, it is this text in John, with its description of the blood and water that flowed from Jesus' side, which is most vividly eucharistic (as well as baptismal) and has been interpreted as such through the centuries. This blood testifies that it is a *'living* sacrifice'.[3] It evokes the new Covenant sealed by the victim Jesus in contrast with the Old Covenant between God and Abraham sealed by animal victims.[4] And, it is a sign of the slain Paschal Lamb in whose red blood our robes are washed white.[5] John is so insistent that his witness is true, and that blood and water both flowed from Jesus' side, because this signifies the reality of the sacrifice.[6] He knows that it is our *believing* that makes it real for us. Both blood and water are purifying and signs of the Spirit, bright and healing as the river of life.[7]

We all know the words which are the pulsing heart of the Gospel: 'God so *loved* the world that He *gave* His only Son. . . .'[8] But perhaps we need to know more fully that God's giving this Son was a giving Him up to death. By His own blood, He has freed us . . . because He loves us.[9] How better can we thank Him than by sharing in this eucharistic sacrifice—especially since *eucharistia* means 'thanksgiving'!

* * *

[1] Galatians 6:14
[2] 1 Corinthians 2:2; Galatians 2:20
[3] Romans 12:1
[4] Genesis 15
[5] 1 Corinthians 5:7; Apocalypse 7:14
[6] 1 John 5:6
[7] John 7:38; Apocalypse 22:1
[8] John 3:16
[9] Apocalypse 1:5

THE CROSS

'Purify me, Father, wash me white—
clean as virgin snow upon the breast
of earth. Purge my past and put to rest
my lost sheep wanderings, my flight
from soft pursuing of Your Hand. Light
my last dark passageways with blessing,
Lord, and let me ask that You refresh
me—something sweet to drink, Love-bright.'

'Child, but you *are* purified. You see
(you must—it is your Creed), I gave My Son
Cross-slain as paschal Lamb, that through
His red sacrifice you might be free—cleansed white to life by
Blood your tongue tastes in Wine—which is My Love for you.'

THE LAKE SHORE
(John 21:9-14)

When the disciples got out of the boat onto the land, they saw a charcoal fire there on the shore with fish lying on it, and bread.

Jesus said to them, 'Bring some of the fish that you have just caught.' So Simon Peter went aboard and hauled the net ashore. It was full of large fish, a hundred and fifty-three of them. And although there were so many, the net was not torn.

Jesus said to them, 'Come and have breakfast.'

Now none of the disciples dared ask Him, 'Who are You?' They knew it was the Lord. Jesus came and took the bread and gave it to them, and so with the fish.

This was now the third time that Jesus was revealed to the disciples after He was raised from the dead.

*   *   *

'Come and have breakfast!'

So beautiful is this story of a simple meal upon the lake-shore that it leaves us hushed and breathless as the dawn sky rising over those still waters. This sky and this shore form the last horizon of John's gospel. And somehow, all the profound and mature reflections of this evangelist upon who Jesus really was and the meaning of His ministry are brought together into this vision of the dawn-lit lakeshore. There we find Him kneeling, in all His humanness, tending a charcoal fire upon the sand. Yes, somehow all the life-giving words which the 'beloved disciple' has given us about the Love of Jesus are contained in His simple call, 'Come, have breakfast.' His great teaching 'Abide in My Love' takes on shape, texture, and warmth in the bread which He holds out to us, hot from the fire upon which He himself has baked it. Yes, this Love takes on a body, gently beating with Life, because in the end this bread is His own flesh. It is Himself.

Technically, this episode, like that of Emmaus, is a 'post-resurrection narrative.' Hence, the meal with the disciples represents not only eucharistic fellowship, but also a 'proof' that the risen Jesus could partake of the same bodily nourishment now as before His death. And the narrative also, of course, is associated with all the other references to fishing throughout the gospels, especially the 'miraculous catch' in Luke.[1] But, no amount of exegesis on this text can ever explain the almost haunting sense of beauty it awakens in us. It makes us feel an almost piercing awareness of our love for Jesus—for this Man who comes so quietly to the disciples (and to all of us) upon the lake shore, offering us warm food after long and cold nights of toil. No added description can define the sense of holy intimacy with Jesus which each personally feels when he realizes that *this*—this humble meal upon the lake shore—is the conclusion God has chosen for the pages of His written gospels.

It was John who had recognized, while they were still far out upon the lake, that the figure standing upon the beach was Jesus. It is John who wrote down what then happened. And so, knowing his sensitivity to his Lord, perhaps we can understand through our eyes why the passage affects us so deeply. In the dawn rising over the calm waters and the grains of sand caressing his feet, in the fire built within a ring of white stones, in the brown-wheated cakes cooking on the flames, . . . and in the gentle Man who tended them and shared freely of this breakfast, John saw his dearest Friend. It was the Friend on whose breast he had lain at the Last Supper. Breaking this bread in the gold glow of morning, John saw anew the Bread upon that table. He saw the Lord who had broken death's fast—with Love.

* * *

[1] Luke 5:1-11

THE LAKE SHORE

Dawn, O dawn broke upon the shore
of Galilee, and He kneeling here
upon the sand . . . and I, standing near
though far out upon the waters, bore
(believing) witness, 'It is He!' For more
than just to give us fish had He appeared
kneeling, dawn-resting. . . . I, endeared
disciple on His breast, knew the Lord's

Supper new-prepared. For when we came
there, cold wet upon the land, we saw
He knelt to shelter (from the night's last
wind) morn's fire, where the flame
kissed alive His Bread, His breath warm:
'Come—take *My* Breakfast, break your fast!'

KOINŌNIA ('FELLOWSHIP', 'COMMUNION')
(Acts 2:44-47)

And all who believed were together and had all things in common. And they sold their possessions and goods and distributed them to all, as any had need.

And day-by-day, attending the temple together and breaking bread in their homes, they partook of food with glad and generous hearts, praising God and having favor with all the people.

And the Lord added to their number day-by-day those who were being saved.

* * *

We have a description here of the first christian community— a picture of their daily life drawn as succinctly and simply as that life itself was simple. And, just because nothing can really be added to this picture, we shall not attempt to interfere with those lines but leave the image they plant in our minds. It is the portrait of a perfect, ideal community having 'all goods in common' and sharing a daily life in which everything was a prayer. We shall marvel above all at the ideal of eucharistic fellowship which is envisaged here: the combination of ordinary meals with Communion Bread in the peoples' homes, the prevailing spirit of glad and generous hearts. Yes, these are the ideals of a christian community. And the verses here comprise one of several such summaries in Acts composed by Luke from his conviction, sensibility, and 'we may presume) observation.

But, the hard facts remain. Whatever he may have believed or observed at the time of his writing, human nature remains timelessly weak. And other writings in the New Testament, even evidence of redactional work in the gospels themselves, indicate that the ideal suffered when bent into practice. The Book of Acts and all the Epistles reveal that factions and divisions, doubts and apostasy, were really in the Church from the beginning. Indeed, Paul tells us that one of the most flagrant abuses against Jesus' commandment of perfect love-fellowship came through the eucharistic celebration itself—which should have been *the* communion![1] But, we do not need to go back to the primitive Church's records to become aware that the once 'glad and generous hearts' have often been replaced by lonely sorrow. We need only to look at the faces of some Christians today. We need only to look at the seemingly hopeless state of divisions in the Church as a whole throughout the ages, not to mention the difficulties of individual Christians in trying to live the demands of Jesus.

But . . . wait! It is not all that hopeless. The 'ideal' is *not* lost or impossible, and nor is this description of the "perfect" early christian community so far from our grasp. For, whatsoever may be our real human weaknesses in 'community', there is One at the heart of it all who *is* 'working all things together for good'.[2] For, 'where two or three are gathered in My name, there am *I* in the midst of them.'[3] Sometimes we can sense this when we look over the horizon at dawn or dusk and see all the steeples raising their crosses against the skyline. We know the comfort that beneath them rests the quiet, alive Wafer Host who is the breathing heart of everything, and whose warm life-Blood

.109

flowing in our veins unites us with one another. We can sense it even more when we look into the horizon of our hearts and find *Him* there, always and all ways—Saviour to our weakness. For, in Jesus, in the very flesh of His Bread, we who are many become one body.[4] He has given His word: there *will* be one flock and One Shepherd.[5]

* * *

[1] 1 Corinthians 11:17-22
[2] Romans 8:28
[3] Matthew 18:20
[4] 1 Corinthians 10:17
[5] John 10:16

KOINŌNIA

Koinōnia—fellowship—it came
so simply then—just communion led
by the sharing of possessions, fed
by the prayers whispered in His name,
by the Temple-teaching . . . and the same
glad *eucharistia*—thanks said—
in every home over broken bread,
table-fellowship . . . *agapē.*

Ah, blessedness blazed beyond hope
seems such a vision, when the ice
binds your closed doorways in today's
winter. . . . No! This Table stays! Open
dawn's secret, when the steeple's sky
Cross shall feed you with the Son's rays.

NEW PASSOVER
(1 Corinthians 5:7f)

Cleanse out the old leaven that you may be a new lump, since you really are unleavened. For Christ, our paschal lamb, has been sacrificed.

Let us, therefore, celebrate the festival not with the old leaven, the leaven of malice and evil, but with the unleavened bread of sincerity and truth.

*   *   *

The Bible is a magical place for finding tiny, shining gems unexpectedly within a vast treasury of other riches. Such is the case here where we find, tucked into Paul's instructions concerning a specific 'case of immorality', one of the most pleasing of texts. It is small (and effective!) as the leaven it describes. It is like a smiling 'Hallelu-jah' sung out from the midst of weightier matters. The synoptics use the image of leaven to symbolize the irresistible growth of the Kingdom from tiny beginnings.[1] Paul, however, by repeating 'a little bit of leaven leavens the whole lump',[2] is referring to the corrupting nature of wickedness. His thoughts on the 'immoral' individual have moved him to lament that even one person in the community will corrode the whole (like a rotting apple!). And this, in turn, leads him to plead that the old leaven be completely purged out, in order that the dough might become new. Now in actual fact, it is not possible to make unleavened bread from leavened—that is, to 'empty out' the leaven from the bread, as it were. But, Paul's point is that the property in leaven which makes it continually expand by feeding on the dough must be rooted out. It must be destroyed. Christians must begin anew.

This is not just a reference 'out of the blue'. Paul is also thinking of the *Torah* regulation that all old leaven must be destroyed before Passover. Only the simpler, unleavened bread may be eaten at the Paschal feast (in memory of the bread which the Hebrews were forced to eat so swiftly on the night of the Exodus.)[3] The Paschal feast was to make purification from the past and new life for the future. It commemorated liberation from bondage. And so, as Paul goes on explicitly to say, the death of Jesus can be seen as the new and true Passover. Through the sacrifice of *this* Paschal Lamb, we are truly liberated into newness of life. Joined to Him, we can be the pure and simple 'unleavened bread' that we really are. Finally, it is possible that Paul's exhortation to the Christians to 'keep the feast' is a reference to the *christian* Passover: Easter, with its eucharistic meal. And so, his tone is one of *joy*. As followers of Jesus, we are to 'rejoice always'[4] because ... *happy* are we who are called to His Supper!

* * *

[1] Luke 13:20f; Matthew 13:31-33
[2] 1 Corinthians 5:6; Galatians 5:9
[3] Exodus 12:15f
[4] Philippians 4:4

NEW PASSOVER

Cleanse, cleanse out the old, begin the new!
The leaven of the past cast off, prize
the unleavened future of the true
Loaf: Christ our Pasch is sacrificed.
Ah, an image hard to grasp? No;
reality, not sign; look to yeast
within your homes: It keeps the old dough
to thrive . . . until purified by feast
of Passover (whose rite recalls a flight
so fast your only bread was leavenless—
dead). And so are you—old life
emptied from you as you stand cleansed
(at death's threshold) waiting new.
                              But lo, the slain

Lamb is risen—Easter noon—yeast for you again!

ONE BODY
(1 Corinthians 10:16f)

The cup of blessing which we bless, is it not participation in the blood of Christ? The bread which we break, is it not a participation in the body of Christ?

Because there is one bread, we who are many are one body, for we all partake of the one bread.

* * *

'Holy *Communion*'—do we ever pause to consider how this word has entered the Church's liturgical vocabulary, let alone what it really means? Its obvious sense is clear enough, even though we may never think of it. It embraces the notion of union—union in prayer with God or in body with Jesus. It may represent whatever way a person experiences that deep oneness, that companionship, which enters our hearts whenever the Bread-wafer and Wine enter our bodies. But, it would be helpful to look more carefully at the background of the term. The actual Greek word is *koinōnia*; we have already mentioned this indirectly in our reflection upon the passage in Acts. It can be translated as 'fellowship', 'participation', or 'communion'. And, this is the word which is used in the Pauline text which we are considering here—a remarkable passage because it states so succinctly such a marvellous teaching as 'communion in the one Body'.

The context will at first seem strange (especially because Paul has a propensity for leaping about from one subject to another). It is actually a delayed continuation of his counsel on the matter of whether or not Christians should eat 'meat sacrificed to idols'. His conclusion before was that, since idols have no existence for a Christian, he is therefore perfectly free to eat such food on social occasions in people's homes (providing he does not offend the conscience of any of his brethren). Here, however, Paul forbids the Christian to eat such food while actually participating in a pagan sacrificial meal, for such an act would make him a 'partner' in pagan worship. But, what is really the prime motive for shunning such idolatrous worship—indeed, the reason for feeling positively *no* attraction to it? It is that Christians have their *own* perfect 'partnership', their *own* 'participation'. The 'cup of blessing' and the 'bread we break' (both phrases used for the Eucharist) are their *koinōnia* in the body of Christ. And this *koinōnia*—this participation—means precisely to become one in this Body by partaking of one bread. This is the very height of union (the union envisaged in a different order by the marriage ideal of husband and wife becoming 'one flesh').[1] It is . . . co-union: Communion.

Now, such a concept is not foreign to us. We have heard of the ideal of contemplative 'mystical union' with God, an experience transcending all earthly senses. We have been taught further of Paul's doctrine on the so-called 'Mystical Body': Jesus is the head of His body the Church, 'the fulness of Him who fills all in all',[2] and we are 'one body in Christ, and individually members one of another.'[3] And, we have experienced an inner union with Jesus in prayer, a union we have yearned to attain perfectly in the Hereafter: '*Marana tha*—Come, Lord Jesus!'[4] All these are very good and real expressions of 'communion'. But, the point is that we are not really compelled to seek it in anything mystical or abstract or beyond the senses. For, *the* Communion—the Fellowship—with Jesus comes through something as tangible and earth-bound as bread and wine! It comes through the flesh of man and the flesh of God, in His Son, becoming one.

* * *

[1] Genesis 2:24; Mark 10:7; 1 Corinthians 6:16; Ephesians 5:31
[2] Ephesians 1:23
[3] Romans 12:5
[4] 1 Corinthians 16:22; Apocalypse 22:20

ONE BODY

Union! When we drink this blessing wine,
break this bread, do we not commune
as one in the Lord's Last Supper room—
more, participate in Him, deep calling unto
deep hope: 'I am coming soon'—
sweet removing of our souls to find

union, mystical beyond our flesh. . . .
Yet, yet mystery! His
live body in this loaf we taste,
His warm blood flows—guest
touchable—within our cups. This
the Union: God enwombed in man . . . chaste!

PAUL'S EUCHARIST
(1 Corinthians 11:23-26)

For I received from the Lord what I also delivered to you: that the Lord Jesus, on the night when He was betrayed, took bread. And when He had given thanks, He broke it, and said, 'This is My Body which is for you. Do this in remembrance of Me.'

In the same way, also the cup after supper, saying, 'This cup is the new covenant in My Blood. Do this, as often as you drink it, in remembrance of Me.'

For as often as you eat this bread and drink the cup, you proclaim the Lord's death until He comes.

* * *

This is one of the most significant passages in the New Testament for the formal 'institution' of the Eucharist. Here we have the familiar eucharistic words which are also found in the synoptics and which have become the center of the Mass. Everything else radiates from these words. Indeed, they *are* the Mass. They represent all that we have been taught about the 'Lord's Supper' or 'Holy Communion'. And whether it has been in Latin or whatever language we speak or even in the unvoiced language of our hearts, we have *always* heard these words before our taking this Bread and Wine. 'This is My body, this My blood: take, eat,

119

drink. . . .' And though we have not understood (for, is it not 'the mystery of faith'?), and though we have only half grasped what it is that we believe, yet we have 'taken and eaten'. We have done this, as He asked, in memory of Jesus.

The passage is significant, too, because of the way in which it is introduced. It indicates the role of tradition in the early Church and how teachings were handed down. For, Paul says that he is telling us what he himself had received. He is delivering to us what had already been delivered to him—by 'the Lord'. Now this does not necessarily mean that Jesus personally revealed to Paul, through a special direct revelation or intimation, the words which then follow. (But who are we to say? Since 'nothing is impossible to God'. . . .) It is more likely that he is thinking of what he had 'received from the Lord' through the body of teachings handed down in the christian community to which he belonged. This means that the 'words of institution' which Paul relates are part of a liturgical formula used in the early Church. And the fact that liturgical practice differed from place-to-place in the different communities of that Church explains why the accounts of what Jesus said at the Last Supper vary slightly. Matthew and Mark follow one pattern, Luke and Paul another. Moreover, seeing that what we call the 'words of institution' in the New Testament was a liturgical formula (and still is such in the Mass), we cannot know exactly what Jesus said in the Upper Room at supper on His last night. We know that He gave us His own body and blood to feed us forever in the form of bread and wine. Yet, the exact words He used then (or any time, for that matter) we cannot really know.

But, we do not really need to know. Our 'knowing' is our believing.[1] And this (as our believing can also tell us) is the way it was for Paul. Yes, this text is significant because of the tradition which he here passes on to us. But, its deeper significance lies in what he himself must have experienced in the Eucharist in order to have written about it at all, here and elsewhere. For, Paul must have known the living Heart of the Bread and the Wine behind these 'formal' words which he recited and wrote. He must have met his living Friend in the Body and Blood behind the 'mystery of faith'. Paul never actually saw Jesus in the flesh in the way that the other disciples did. But, on the road to Damascus, he beheld Him in a way so profound and so powerful that forever afterwards he knew himself to be in the living presence of his Lord and Friend. And wheresoever Paul's ministry took him, in whatsoever churches he founded, he saw Jesus anew in the flesh of the Bread and the blood of the Wine.

*   *   *

[1] John 6:69

PAUL'S EUCHARIST

Tradition tells the Supper story: He,
the night before a kiss betrayed Him, took bread,
blessed His Abba, gave, and bade, 'Eat,
This is My Body' . . . warmed a cup, said,
'Drink, My blood!' And love (unknowingly) lit
the upper room that night they supped and shared—
so fully men they could not grasp that it
was Man they ate. . . . But I, though missing there
(and though the last of all apostles), know:
Damascus road, He grasped (and kissed) a Saul
to Paul. And ever since, when I would go
(for Him) the long world's roads, all

the homes of Him would share the bread and wine again.
And I (believing) ate my Lord . . . and met my Friend.

UNTRUE TO THE LORD
(1 Corinthians 11:27-29)

Whoever, therefore, eats the bread or drinks the cup of the Lord in an unworthy manner will be guilty of profaning the body and blood of the Lord. Let a man examine himself, and so eat of the bread and drink of the cup. For anyone who eats and drinks without discerning the body eats and drinks judgment upon himself.

* * *

'Guilty of the Lord's body'—perish the thought! What *does* Paul mean? We must look first at the historical context of this entire 'eucharistic section' in 1 Corinthians 11. It is with a critical attitude that Paul introduces the subject in the first place. He finds it needful to correct certain abuses which had crept in to the early christian worship commemorating the Last Supper. He has heard that what would be the community's most perfect bond of unity had become the source of disunity and faction. The custom of sharing an ordinary meal (the *agapē* or 'love feast') *before* the traditional eucharistic service had gotten out of hand. Not only were people capitalizing upon the *agapē* part; far worse, even *that* was not carried out in a spirit of loving unity because each person fended for himself, some remaining hungry while others became drunk. Paul laments chastisingly: 'When you meet together, it is *not* the Lord's Supper that you eat!'[1] (This, by the way, is the only explicit occurrence of the phrase 'The Lord's Supper'—*to kuriakon deipnon*—in the New Testament.) It is this criticism which moves Paul to then relate the tradition according to which the *true* Eucharist was instituted, as we have seen.

Thus, taking the bread or cup of the Lord 'in an unworthy manner' must be seen in this context. One is 'guilty' if he goes to the Communion table in such a state (either physically on account of drunkenness, or spiritually on account of unrest) that he is unable to 'discern' that it *is* the Body and Blood of Jesus of which he is partaking. For reasons different from those Paul had in mind, the Christian of today may be technically 'guilty' according to the 'law'—or, at least, may feel such. But, there is another side of 'guilt' which is more painfully real than could ever be legalized or defined. And this is that secret sorrow of the heart which knows its own weakness, knows the sense of being worthless and failing in love, and hence also knows deep fear. It is that voiceless cry, 'Heal me, O Lord, and I shall be healed; save me and I shall be saved.'[2] And this cry is all the more fearful and anguished because we do not dare, or even know how, ever to voice it.

But, it is at this very point that we hear the comforting refrain of Jesus: 'Fear not!' Paul knew. He came to rejoice in his weakness as his greatest strength because it was then that he was closest to his Lord.[3] And so, Paul must also have known that, if Jesus is the very *first* to relieve all 'guilt', also the very first place He would cast out all fear is when we approach the altar for the Bread and the Wine which He gives. For, if we feel we have failed in love and denied Jesus, it is in this Eucharist that we can most experience how there is *no* fear in *love.* His perfect Love casts out *all* fear.[4] No one knew more keenly than Peter that heart-rending grief of unworthiness and denial. He knew this even to the point of desperate tears. But, we can learn to say as he did: 'Lord, *you* know everything. You *know* that I *love* you!'[5]

*   *   *

[1] 1 Corinthians 11:20
[2] Jeremiah 17:14
[3] 2 Corinthians 12:7-10
[4] 1 John 4:18
[5] John 21:17

UNTRUE TO THE LORD

'Guilty of the Lord's Body', Paul
has written, 'if you eat unworthily
this bread and wine.' Guilt—what did he mean?
Not the chain of Law prescribing all
behaviour which, assuming none must fall,
looms a stumbling stone. Nor did he
mean fear that God (more often, man) would see
something so shameful one were called

outcast from the Table Fellowship.
No: Paul (cast in weakness) saw
the last secret held by pain-sweet
burning in us—Love—that hidden-lipped
denial: 'I untrue—O, heal Lord!'
. . . And He, turning, smiles: 'Take and eat.'

PURE MILK
(1 Peter 2:2f)

*Like newborn babes, long for the pure spiritual milk, that
by it you may grow up to salvation. For you have tasted
the Kindness of the Lord.*

* * *

Milk! Pure Milk!! It is so white against the night when dawn
finds it fresh upon our doorsteps. Milk—what place could
this possibly have in a little book about the Bread and
Wine? It has as much place as the Mother of that Bread had
in His life, and that shall be *our* 'little way' or understanding this text. In two other places in the New Testament,
milk is found as a metaphor for spiritual teaching. In both
of them, it represents the food of 'babes' who have much to
learn in contrast with the more spiritually mature who are
ready for 'solid food'.[1] (Yet who of us is *not* a babe in this
regard. . . ?) In 1 Peter, however, it represents that pure
flow of the christian message for which we all know an
inner 'craving'. It is our hunger and thirst for Jesus Himself,
in whom we have tasted *all* the loving-kindness of God. And
He satisfies that longing through the Bread and the Wine of
His Body and Blood.

But, is there not a point (though, granted, a very quiet
point—hidden from all eyes but those of little ones) at
which this 'milk', with its figurative meaning of Jesus'
teaching, can also be taken literally as the food in the

127

breasts which suckled Him? Yes, Mary's milk! that which alone can satisfy our craving for all that is pure and simple (for, yes, who of us is not a babe. . .). And just as the Bread and the Wine represent the person of Jesus Himself, so does this Milk represent the whole of her. She is Mary, the woman through whom we come to Jesus. She is the Mother who teaches us to eat His white Bread because we first have been little enough to sip the whiter milk of her breast.

* * *

[1] 1 Corinthians 3:2f; Hebrews 5:12-14

PURE MILK

Moon, crescent moon, curved breast
and womb—fruitfulness of motherhood.
How could God give His flesh as food unless
first through woman fed? Hence, how could
there be the Bread, the Wine, unless first
through milk? O mystery—learn of Me,
little children. Turn to Child once nursed
to Life by pure white lily stream.
Turn . . . and yearn yourselves this Milk: Mary.
For *she* it is behind My Bread and Wine:
before you eat Me, you must seek her there
where crescent moon (reflecting Son's sign—

world's light) was womb of mind and white breast
I sucked. There, you shall sup with Me to rest.

HIDDEN MANNA
(Apocalypse 2:17)

To him who conquers I will give some of the hidden manna. And I will give him a white stone, with a new name written on the stone which no one knows except him who receives it.

* * *

What *is* this—'hidden manna'? It occurs in a phrase so tiny and hidden in the Apocalypse that few know it is even there! Perhaps we should ask instead: what did the author have in mind when describing such a thing (since clearly no one can know what it actually is)? Our answer can come only through suggested associations. The manna which God fed His people in the desert appears under different descriptions throughout the Old Testament. In the New Testament, the only other references to 'manna' apart from this one are in the Johannine Bread of Life discourse and in the book of Hebrews, where the Ark of the Covenant is described as having contained a golden urn to hold the manna.[1] It was believed that Jeremiah had taken this Ark, the sacred tent, and the altar of incense and sealed them for safekeeping into a cave near Mt. Nebo. This place was to be 'unknown until God gathers His people together again and shows His mercy.'[2] Perhaps this is what gave rise to the first century 'apocalyptic notion' that the manna, hidden in heaven, would come down at the 'end time' and nourish

Israel. For, it was at the 'end time' that the great 'gathering of the peoples' was to take place.

However, whatever the exact reference in Jewish and Hellenistic circles, the christian author of the Apocalypse certainly must have had in mind the idea of a 'new life' hidden in Jesus Himself. He also must have been thinking of the hidden mysteries associated with His person which would not be revealed until the 'end time'. (And one of those 'mysteries', of course—indeed, perhaps the greatest—is that of the Eucharist or 'heavenly manna'.) As Paul aptly and succinctly expresses it: 'You have died, and your life is hidden with Christ in God.'[3] This interpretation is strengthened by the image in the second part of the 'hidden manna' verse. There we read about a 'white stone' with a 'new name' written upon it. This reflects the custom of the time whereby people wore amulets inscribed with a secret name. When this name was invoked, they believed themselves protected from evil spirits. But, *this* stone in the Apocalypse is *white*—symbolizing the victorious Easter life. And *this* name is new—symbolizing the Victor Himself and His 'new creation'. This is the name which none but Himself can read and which is the *only* means of salvation.[4] The gift of manna and the stone both imply the granting of nourishment and protection for Life's journey.

But, to whom are they given? To him who, like their Giver, has 'overcome'[5] —has held fast His word throughout this life and so entered into the fulness of the next. What, then, *is* this 'hidden manna'? Yes, it is related to the Exodus bread and to the Bread of the Last Supper which Jesus still gives to us in the thin-Love wafer of Communion which becomes our whole daily strength. But, it is even more fully the Bread of the new 'Exodus' to come. At that time, we shall rise as He rose—the Morning Star[6] —to sup with Him face-to-face. The very title 'Apocalypse' signifies the 'revelation' of *all* that has been hidden. The 'hidden manna' is Jesus Himself, 'the mystery hidden for ages . . . now made manifest.'[7]

* * *

[1] Hebrews 9:4
[2] 2 Maccabees 2:4-8
[3] Colossians 3:3
[4] Apocalypse 3:12; 19:12
[5] John 16:33
[6] Luke 1:78f; Apocalypse 2:28, 22:16
[7] Colossians 1:26

HIDDEN MANNA

Hidden manna. . . . I shall give to him
who overcomes a new name—and
hidden manna. Do you understand?
No, a parable, you murmur—dim
hid as this Man! And you limn
different pictures—Moses with the camp
fed in the desert, or a lamp
keeping vigil o'er a chapel's thin

Wafer Host. But not, not these—
not even these—the meal I meant,
my hidden manna . . . but the Morning Star
(I am) feeding you the Bread Easter—
freed beyond death, where you are sent
the secret opening *Maranatha.*

OPENING THE DOOR
(Apocalypse 3:20)

'Behold, I stand at the door and knock.

If any one hears My voice and opens the door, I will come in to him and eat with him, and he with Me.'

* * *

It is so in keeping with the paradox of the whole Bible that the weakest, most wayward city should be the recipient of some of the most sensitive and tender words in the Apocalypse! Jesus—Love Himself—is yearning to be received into their midst. And He offers this invitation to enter their door and 'sup' with them because first He has given His reason for chastising them. 'Those whom I *love* I reprove and chasten'.[1] Laodicea is the last-named city in the beginning section of the Apocalypse containing the 'letters to the seven churches'. It was a center in Asia Minor which was famous for its industry (specializing in woolen garments), its medical school and eye-ointments, and its neighboring mineral hot-springs. The seer is told to relay Jesus' condemnation to this people. He finds them to be the very opposite spiritually of what they purport to be materially. 'You say "I am rich, I have prospered, and I need nothing". But you do not know that you are wretched, pitiable, poor, blind, and naked!'[2] These people are not even cold or hot—but only lukewarm! It is the height of all self-righteous refusal to acknowledge dependency on God. It is a total lack of definite commitment. They have forgotten that it is *God* alone who can clothe them in the whitest of garments and heal their blindness with His salve.

But, the ignorance and faults of Laodicea only stir God's deeper love for them, and it is to *them* that Jesus offers this exquisite invitation to share a meal with Him. It is a continuation of His 'table-fellowship' with the poor and sinful, His inviting people such as these to partake of meals with Him.[3] Since sharing a meal signified harmony and serenity before men and God, this invitation represents Jesus' infinite forgiveness—His solicitude for the 'lost sheep'. And, of course, it must be an indirect reference to the eucharistic supper to which they are invited. At the door of their hearts, Jesus is standing . . . knocking . . waiting. . . .

Yes, Waiting. . . . This is the whole thrust of the verse for us. For, as Jesus stands at our thresholds knocking, it is up to us to hear Him and *open* the door. And once *we* have opened, He will not hesitate to come in and eat with us and we with Him. It is the Bread and Wine of Communion that He offers us, yes. But, we can grasp this reality only if we first understand what it is like to have Him with us breaking a simpler bread. And we understand this best, sometimes, through the pain of not having Him which we often feel. It is a hollow ache within us, even though our lives may be contented and fruitful, for Another at our sides. For, we sense that 'something (Someone) is missing'. But, out of this lonely emptiness, after traversing the long fields of the day and coming to rest beside the silent hearth fire, a knock comes. A knock comes—and suddenly we are no longer alone . . . if we but open the door, if we but open. If we could only open our heart to Him, suddenly we are no longer empty. For Jesus enters, sups with us, and 'fills the hungry with good things':[4] Himself.

135

* * *

[1] Apocalypse 3:19
[2] Apocalypse 3:17
[3] Matthew 11:19; Luke 15:2; Mark 2:15f
[4] Luke 1:53

OPENING THE DOOR

'Betimes, Lord, it seems that something far
is lost and missing midst the rich loam
of wheatfields in the evening mist, when home
harkens footsteps through the harvest dark
hoping warmth, friendship, and (ah, hard
earned) daily bread. And yet, although
the hearth glow there is Love, alone
the loaf I seem to break: You seem apart.'

'No! Do you not hear when I stand
here, at your door, knocking, waiting
you to answer, open, offer bread—
My Supper? Do you not yet understand?
This Love-Wheat you hunger—I! And breaking,
you in Me (and I in you) are fed.'

CALLED TO HIS SUPPER
(Apocalypse 19:9)

Happy are they who are called to the marriage supper of the Lamb!

* * *

The marriage supper of the Lamb! The Apocalypse contains the message of the entire Bible in the small space of its pages (even as Mary contained in the small space of her womb the Saviour of the whole world. . .). Here we have a vision of that final eschatological fulfilment whose promise is a 'golden thread' woven throughout the Bible. Indeed, both the promise *and* fulfilment of that Final Day become enfleshed in the Man behind the Gospel. One of the themes included in this promise is that of the final Meal, the 'eschatological banquet', to be shared in the Father's Kingdom. The Old Testament refers to this in quite a general way in those passages which envisage an abundance of food and drink in the End Time. Everyone who thirsts is to come to the great Waters to buy wine and milk without price and bread which truly satisfies.[1] For, in the last days, 'the mountains shall drip sweet wine, and the hills shall flow with milk and all the streambeds of Judah shall flow with water.'[2] The New Testament makes the theme more specific in the references to an actual eschatological banquet. The poor, the maimed, the blind, and the lame shall be summoned to this wedding feast.[3] Many shall come from

East and West to sup with the Father.[4] And the disciples who have borne with Jesus in His trials are promised a place in His Kingdom, so that they may eat and drink at His table.[5] Yes, 'Blessed—happy—is he who shall eat bread in the kingdom of God!'[6]

However, it is not entirely in the future. For, to eat bread in the Kingdom of God is not a vague hope, but a definite promise which is already fulfilled in 'table-fellowship' with His Son. This fellowship, a foretaste of the heavenly banquet, began when Jesus shared meals with 'the poor'. He dined with all those who were the outcasts and the down-trodden and the 'sinners' in society. His acting thus in the face of all the disapproval of the time was the clearest demonstration of God's merciful Love and saving forgiveness. And, of course, Jesus continues to offer this 'table-fellowship' at the altar table, in Communion with Him (and with one another) in the Bread and the Wine. This Union He has given in order to nourish us 'as we wait in joyful hope for His coming', as it says after the Consecration in the Mass. This refers to that perfect sharing, face-to-face, when He comes to us and sups with us, and we with Him, in resurrection. At the hour when He gave us this food, Jesus said that, although He would not be eating or drinking again on this earth, He would do so anew in His Father's Kingdom. The Last Supper (and the Cross that had to follow) *would* lead to the Marriage Supper.

The Apocalypse takes up the pictorial language, as well as the themes, of the entire Bible. And so, there is somehow a special poignancy in this image: He who has called Himself the Good Shepherd of the poor and has fed His lambs in green pastures and laid a table for them in the presence of their fears—*this* Shepherd becomes, at His own Marriage Supper, a Lamb! The conquering 'lion of the tribe of Judah' becomes the Paschal Lamb who was slain for us.

And through this, He became enthroned to lead us anew as a Shepherd in our midst.[7] It is *He* whom we must follow wherever He goes.[8] We must follow Him above all to the Marriage Supper. There the Jerusalem whose milk is our warm consolation[9] becomes His bride, and they feed us—little lambs—with Bread and Wine.

'Happy, O happy are *we* who are called to His Supper!'

* * *

[1] Isaiah 55:1-3
[2] Joel 3:18
[3] Luke 14:15-24; Matthew 22:1-10
[4] Matthew 8:11
[5] Luke 22:28-30
[6] Luke 14:15
[7] Apocalypse 5:5f; 7:17
[8] Apocalypse 14:4
[9] Isaiah 66:10f; Apocalypse 19:7f; 21:2

CALLED TO HIS SUPPER

Though the centuries stream stark and long
unending, little children, when the wheat
you toil with sweating brow can never meet
the multitudes hungering for strong
life staff—bread,—to belong
to your todays, fear not! Sweet
the yoke of My tomorrow which completes
your waiting days with song—it shan't be long!

The poor, the hungry, and the little one,
forever empty, forever crying to be fed—
ah, these you shall always see (and are . . .).
But I, Shepherd feeding, am begun
to bid you to the Lamb's Supper—Bread
in the Kingdom of My Morning Star!

FINIS: 'FEAR NOT!'

*   *   *

And so, all these biblical texts have shown us how we have been called to the Lamb's Supper . . . and why we are thus to be happy. At this Supper we are given Bread to satisfy *all* hunger (for we hunger for many things) and Wine to hush all thirst.[1]

But we remain only little lambs at this our Shepherd's meal. And life is as real for us as it was for Him. Sometimes we cannot know this happiness of being there with Him in the Breaking of the Bread. Instead, we know fear and pain . . . and death. And sometimes, the little candle of Believing which we would carry lighted to His Table flickers beneath the rain (our tears) of the Night.

But listen, listen! Does not the Shepherd *know* His sheep and understand?[2] He does not save us *from* the Night, no, but He *does* lead us safely *through* it. His light shines in the darkness, but the darkness cannot overcome it. . . .[3]

'Fear not, little flock!
Your Father is joyed to give you this Kingdom,
that you might feed at My Supper both Now
and Forever.[4]

Did I not tell you (do you *still* not understand?)—
If you eat of Me, you shall not die. You shall Live.
For I am living bread, the Bread of *Life*![5]

And so, in your darkest hour, look outwards
through your window,

142

dip your candle into Dawn
to be lit by the hearth fire warming Bread
in the Morning Star.
It is *I*!'[6]

* * *

[1] John 6:35
[2] John 10:14, 27
[3] John 1:5
[4] Luke 12:32
[5] Psalm 118:17; John 6:48-51
[6] Apocalypse 2:28; 22:16

FEAR NOT!

I am afraid, Lord—there! Small
words (encompassing so much) . . . but now
that I have spoken, I can tell you how
frightened I (timid lamb) fall
when my candle flickers and the tall
forest of the Unforeseen bows
black shadows on my babe's brow . . .
and I afraid of the Night's call.

Fear not, little flock! I,
Shepherd, once was Lamb Paschal-slain
to save you—not to save from the night,
but lead your passages to My dawn-sky's
pasture. Patience—Follow, unafraid!
Darkness cannot overcome My Light.